Beaches of Kaua'i and Ni'ihau

Beaches of Kaua'i
and Ni'ihau

John R. K. Clark

A KOLOWALU BOOK
University of Hawaii Press
Honolulu

04 03 02 01   6 5 4 3

Library of Congress Cataloging-in-Publication Data

Clark, John R. K., 1946–
    Beaches of Kauaʻi and Niʻihau / John R. K. Clark.
        p.   cm. — (A Kolowalu book)
    Bibliography: p.
    Includes index.
    ISBN 0–8248–1260–3 (alk. paper)
        1.   Kauai County (Hawaii)—Description and travel—Guide-books.
    2.   Niihau (Hawaii)—Description and travel—Guide-books.
    3.   Beaches—Hawaii—Kauai County—Guide-books.   4.   Beaches—
    Hawaii—Niihau—Guide-books.   I.   Title.
    DU628.K3C58   1989   89–36116
    919.69'4044–dc20   CIP

"Kīpū Kai" by Mary Kawena Pukui reprinted with permission

Photo Credits
Cover: Donkey Beach, Kauaʻi, by John Bowen
Title page: Poʻooneone Beach, Niʻihau, by Steve Russell
Kauaʻi: photos by John Bowen
Niʻihau: photos by John Bowen and Steve Russell

The real value of [these] contributions to the written history and antiquities of ancient Hawaii is something that must be left for appraisal to the historian, the critic and student of Hawaiian affairs. The lapse of years will no doubt sensibly appreciate this valuation, as well as the regret, which many even at the present time feel most keenly, that more was not saved from the foundering bark of ancient Hawaii. If the student has to mourn the loss of bag and baggage, he may at least congratulate himself on the saving of a portion of the scrip and scrippage—half a loaf is better than no bread.

Hawaiian Antiquities
David Malo, 1898

Contents

Maps   ix

Preface   xi

Acknowledgments   xiii

Beaches of Kaua'i

Niumalu Beach Park   2
Nāwiliwili Park (Small Boat Harbor)   2
Kalapakī Beach   3
Ninini Beach   5
Ahukini State Recreation Pier   5
Hanamā'ulu Beach Park   6
Nukoli'i Beach Park   6
Lydgate State Park   7
Wailua Beach   8
Waipouli Beach   9
Kapa'a Beach Park   10
Keālia Beach   11
Donkey Beach   12
Anahola Beach Park   14
'Aliomanu Beach   14
Pāpa'a Bay   16
Moloa'a Bay   16
Larsens Beach   17
Pīla'a Beach   18
Waiakalua Iki Beach   20
Waiakalua Nui Beach   21
Kāhili Beach   21
Kīlauea Point National Wildlife Refuge   22
Kauapea Beach   23
Kalihiwai Beach   24
'Anini Beach Park   24

Princeville   26
Black Pot Beach Park   27
Hanalei Pavilion Beach Park   29
Wai'oli Beach Park   30
Waikoko Beach   30
Lumaha'i Beach   32
Wainiha Beach Park   34
Kepuhi Beach   35
Tunnels Beach   36
Hā'ena Beach Park   36
Hā'ena State Park   37
Nā Pali Coast State Park   40
Hanakāpī'ai Beach   41
Kalalau Beach   42
Honopū Beach   44
Nu'alolo Kai Beach   45
Miloli'i Beach   47
Polihale State Park   49
Pacific Missile Range Facility   50
Kekaha Beach Park   52
Kīkīaola Small Boat Harbor   53
Waimea State Recreation Pier   54
Lucy Wright Beach Park   54
Pākalā Beach   56
Salt Pond Beach Park   58
Hanapēpē Beach Park   59
Port Allen   59
Wahiawa Bay   60
Kalāheo   61
Pālama Beach   62
Lāwa'i Kai   64
Spouting Horn Beach Park   65

Kukui‘ula Small Boat Harbor   65
Beach House Beach   66
Prince Kūhiō Park   67
Kōloa Landing   68
Po‘ipū Beach   68
Wai‘ōhai Beach   69
Po‘ipū Beach Park   71
Brennecke Beach   71
Shipwreck Beach   72
Māhā‘ulepū Beach   73
Kīpū Kai   76

Beaches of Ni‘ihau

Keamano Beach   80
Ka‘aku‘u Beach   81
Keawanui Beach   84

Kauwaha Beach   86
Pu‘uwai Beach   88
Ki‘eki‘e Beach   92
Nonopapa Beach   92
Kamalino Beach   94
Keanahaki Beach   96
Po‘ooneone Beach   98
Kalaoa Beach   99
Pōleho Beach   100

Water Safety   103

Ocean Recreation Activities   107

References   109

Index   113

Maps

Kaua'i

1. Kaua'i   1
2. Nāwiliwili   3
3. Anahola   10
4. Kīlauea   19
5. Hā'ena   30
6. Nā Pali Coast   37
7. Polihale   47
8. Kekaha   52
9. Hanapēpē   56
10. Po'ipū   62
11. Kīpū Kai   76

Ni'ihau

1. Ni'ihau   79
2. Keawanui   80
3. Pu'uwai   87
4. Po'ooneone   93
5. Kalaoa   99

Preface

Beaches of Kaua'i and Ni'ihau is the final volume of a four-volume series on Hawaiian beaches. With the completion of this book every beach on the eight major Hawaiian islands has been inventoried and described. Like its predecessors, *The Beaches of O'ahu, The Beaches of Maui County,* and *Beaches of the Big Island,* this book offers a physical and historical sketch of each beach on the islands, provides information on beach activities, and details water safety concerns.

The island of Kaua'i, one of the oldest of the eight major islands, has more sand beach per mile of shoreline than any of the other seven islands. White sand beaches comprise 50 miles or 44 percent of Kaua'i's 113 miles of shoreline, almost twice the percentage of O'ahu, its closest rival. Kaua'i is popularly known as The Garden Island in recognition of its lushly vegetated mountains and valleys, but it should be even more widely renowned for its many beautiful beaches, one of its greatest and probably least acknowledged attractions.

The longest and widest beaches are located on the north and west coasts and are heavily used by beachgoers. These coasts are also subject to high surf during the winter and spring, and most of Kaua'i's drownings and near-drownings occur at remote and unguarded beaches on these shores. One of goals of this book is to forewarn people who visit these beaches of the dangers they may encounter and to remind them that they must assume responsiblity for their own actions. People who act irresponsibly may suddenly find themselves in a life-threatening situation.

The island of Ni'ihau is privately owned by the Robinson family of Kaua'i. Ever since the Robinsons have owned Ni'ihau, the island has had an aura of mystery to the rest of the world, the kind of mystery attached to most forbidden places; the family has maintained a strict closed-door policy, prohibiting entry to anyone who is not a resident of the island, a member of the Robinson family, or an invited guest. Although the Robinsons conduct helicopter tours for the public to Ni'ihau, they do not allow any contact between the visitors and the native Hawaiians on the island.

Ni'ihau is 15 miles across the Kaulakahi Channel from Kaua'i. The only visitors to the island and its surrounding waters are fishermen and sailors. Although Ni'ihau has many beautiful beaches, the Robinsons discourage outsiders from landing. By state law all beaches in the Hawaiian Islands are public property up to the vegetation line, but Ni'ihau's owners believe that their deed gives them title to the beaches as well as the lands above them. In a newspaper article in the *Honolulu Advertiser* of October 29, 1988, Bruce Robinson stated, "Our deed very clearly leads to the water. It is a separate deed quite unique in Hawaii. It stems directly from the monarchy, and with it comes the aboriginal rights of the old days." To date the Robinsons' claims of private beach ownership have not been challenged in a court of law by anyone who has been asked to leave the island.

The material in *Beaches of Kaua'i and Ni'ihau* is a blend of information from many sources, including the literature mentioned in the References, interviews with the informants listed in the Acknowledgments, and my personal observations at each beach. Anyone who is interested in additional information about any part of the book may contact me through the publisher.

Acknowledgments

During the three-year period spent in gathering material for *Beaches of Kaua'i and Ni'ihau,* I interviewed many individuals, either in person, by mail, or by telephone, and was assisted in various capacities by many more. The information and help they provided was invaluable. I would like to recognize the following people whose contributions were of major importance:

John Akana, Abraham Akuna, John Alford, Pat Bacon, Linda Bail, Alex Beck, Nick Beck, Beryl and Gary Blaich, Suzanne Bollin, David Boynton, Jean Brady, Marvin Brennecke, Barbara Brundage, Betty Bushnell, George Christian, Barlow Chu, Chris Cook, Charlie Cowden, Dougie Davidson, Carter Davis, Don Donohugh, Kippy Dunbar, Pat Durkin, Rex Elliott, Bill Enoka, Edna Estrellas, John Fink, Bill Fleming, Skipper Forrest, Donna Garcia, Henry Gomez, Kaipo Ho, Scott Hoepfl, Bill Huddy, Wade Ishikawa, Chris Kainard, Gordon Kaluahine Sr., Ann Kawamoto, and Stuart Kiang.

Sammy Lee, Wayne Lovell, Jim and Lorre Lucas, David Maki, Mike Markrich, Donald Kilolani Mitchell, Ralph Moberly, Bob Moncrief, James Morgan, Don Moses, Michelle Moses, Michael Mundon, Phil Myer, John Naughton, Roy Niino, Ann Marie Norton, Dustin O'Halloran, Terry O'Halloran, Annie Orcutt, William Panui, Pat Phillips, Alan Rietow, Steve Russell, Larry Sasaki, Chad Schimmelfenning, Cheryl Sherman, Carol Silva, Sybil Solis, David Sproat, Wayne Souza, Elise Taylor, Sona Taylor, Thayne Taylor, Robert Thomas, Henry Thronas, Billie Smith Topp, Kathy Valier, Mel Ventura, Ron Wagner, Randy Weir, Carol Wilcox, C. B. Wilson, Martha Yent, Aaron Young, and Kalani Young.

I would also like to recognize the following people whose encouragement, help, and support made the completion of this book possible: Paul Bartram, John Bowen, Jason Clark, Kiki Mookini, Donald, Hannah, Mary, Linda, and Dan Moriarty, Alice and Larry Stanley, and Julie Ushio.

Island of Kaua'i

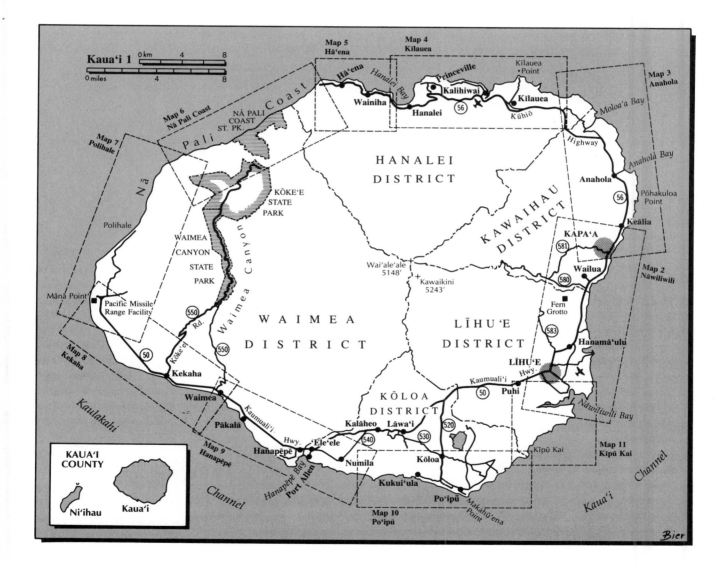

Kaua'i 1

0 km   4   8
0 miles   4   8

Map 5
Hā'ena

Map 4
Kīlauea

Kīlauea
• Point

Map 3
Anahola

Hā'ena   Hanalei Bay   Princeville

Kalihiwai

Map 6
Nā Pali Coast

NĀ PALI
COAST
ST. PK.

Wainiha   Hanalei   Kīlauea

Kūhiō   56

Moloa'a Bay

Map 7
Polihale

Nā Pali Coast

KŌKE'E
STATE
PARK

HANALEI
DISTRICT

Highway

Anahola

Anahola Bay

Polihale

WAIMEA
CANYON
STATE
PARK

KAWAIHAU
DISTRICT

Pōhakuloa
Point

56

Keālia

KAPA'A

581

Wai'ale'ale
5148'

Wailua

Māna Point

Pacific Missile
Range Facility

550

Waimea Canyon

+ Kawaikini
5243'

WAIMEA

DISTRICT

Fern
Grotto

580

Map 2
Nāwiliwili

550

LĪHU'E
DISTRICT

583

Hanamā'ulu

Map 8
Kekaha

50

Kōke'e Rd.

LĪHU'E

Kaumuali'i   Hwy.

Kekaha

Puhi   50

Waimea

Kaumuali'i

KŌLOA
DISTRICT

Nāwiliwili Bay

Kaulakahi

Pākalā

Hwy.

Kalāheo   Lāwa'i

520

Map 11
Kīpū Kai

Map 9
Hanapēpē

'Ele'ele   540   530

Kīpū Kai

Hanapēpē

Numila

Kōloa

KAUA'I
COUNTY

Hanapēpē Bay   Port Allen

Kukui'ula

Po'ipū

Channel

Makāhū'ena
Point

Kaua'i
Channel

Ni'ihau   Kaua'i

Channel

Map 10
Po'ipū

Bier

Niumalu Beach Park

Aloha ‘ia no au Līhu‘e
I ka ne‘e mai a ka ua Paupili.

Ua pili no au me ku‘u aloha
Me ke kau nehe mai au Niumalu.

Beloved is Līhu‘e
When the Paupili rain comes.

I cling to my beloved
Under the soft rustling [leaves] of Niumalu.

"Līhu‘e"
Traditional song

Niumalu is a small residential community on the shore of Nāwiliwili Harbor. It was once the home of Paul Kanoa, a former governor of Kaua‘i. Born in South Kona in 1802, Kanoa was appointed governor of Kaua‘i in 1847 and held the position until May 10, 1877, when he resigned. He died in 1885. Today, approximately forty families live in Niumalu; fishing and farming are part of their rural life-style.

Immediately inland of Niumalu on the Hulē‘ia River is Menehune Fishpond, one of Kaua‘i's most famous landmarks. This ancient pond, historically known as Alekoko, was formed by the construction of a 2,700-foot-long stone wall that cut off a bend in the river. It is one of the most archaeologically important fishponds on Kaua‘i and is so old that its construction is attributed to the Menehune, a mythical people who reputedly inhabited Hawai‘i before the arrival of the Hawaiians. Menehune Fishpond is also considered to be the best remaining example of an inland fishpond in the state.

Adjoining Menehune Fishpond is the Hulē‘ia National Wildlife Refuge, 238 acres of river basin and steep, heavily wooded slopes in Hulē‘ia Valley. The refuge was established in 1973. Its seasonally flooded flats and the Hulē‘ia River estuary provide habitat for four species of endangered waterbirds, the *āe‘o* or Hawaiian stilt, the *‘alae ke‘oke‘o* or Hawaiian coot, the *‘alae ‘ula* or Hawaiian gallinule, and the *koloa maoli* or Hawaiian duck. This area once supported a community of native Hawaiians who raised wetland taro in a still visible series of terraces and irrigation ditches.

The fishpond and refuge are visible from Hulemalu Road, but they are not open to the public. The fishpond is privately owned, but the refuge is federal property, managed by the U.S. Fish and Wildlife Service. Both may also be seen from the Hulē‘ia River, a navigable river that is accessible from either Nāwiliwili Harbor or Niumalu Beach Park.

Niumalu Beach Park is a small park bordering the inner reaches of Nāwiliwili Harbor. A narrow boat ramp in the park is used to launch and land small, shallow-draft boats. The bay bottom fronting the ramp is a muddy tidal flat, and the surrounding shoreline is overgrown with mangrove and a few *milo* trees. The park is very popular with local picnickers and campers. Shoreline fishing, crabbing, and net fishing are common pastimes.

The park is also bordered by Hulē‘ia River which is used by small boat fishermen for fishing and crabbing. Kayakers, windsurfers, jetskiers, and waterskiers also use the river. In former times the Niumalu area and the rest of Nāwiliwili Bay supported an important mullet fishery, but heavy siltation in the bay and other habitat damage have apparently caused the decline of the industry. Net fishermen report that the Hulē‘ia River estuary is also a spawning ground for sharks, particularly hammerheads, and many juvenile sharks are inadvertently netted in the bay areas, especially during the summer months.

Nāwiliwili Park

Kaulana mai nei a o Nāwiliwili
He nani no ‘oe nā milimili
He beauty maoli no.

Famous is Nāwiliwili
Your beauty is greatly admired
A genuine beauty.

"Nāwiliwili"
Traditional song

Nāwiliwili means "the *wiliwili* trees." These trees provided the Hawaiians with orange-to-red seeds that were strung into leis and a very light wood that was used to make surfboards, canoe outriggers, and fishnet floats. Once plentiful on the mountain slopes above the southern side of Nāwiliwili Harbor, only a few of these important native trees can be found in the area today.

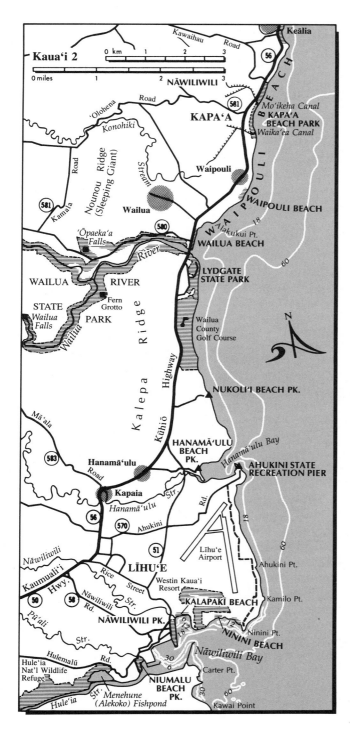

One of two commercial deep-water ports on Kaua'i, Nāwiliwili Harbor is the island's principal port, accommodating a wide range of vessels including passenger liners, interisland barges, freighters, and tankers. The harbor was first surveyed for a port for the Hawaiian government in 1881 by George Jackson, but construction of a breakwater and a turning basin was not authorized by Congress until 1919. During construction of the harbor, a retaining wall was built along the water's edge, and spoil material from dredging of the basin was deposited inland of the wall to enlarge the waterfront. The harbor was officially opened to commercial shipping on July 22, 1930. Its first caller was the *Hualālai,* an interisland passenger and cargo vessel.

On the south side of the commercial harbor is Nāwiliwili Small Boat Harbor with a berthing capacity for 160 vessels. Harbor facilities include a boat ramp, restrooms, and parking for automobiles and trailers. Both recreational and commercial vessels utilize the site, which is also a favorite spot for shoreline fishermen.

On the north side of the commercial harbor is Nāwiliwili Park. The entire seaward edge of this long, narrow park is formed by a concrete sea wall. The primary park activities are picnicking, fishing, and surfing. The surfing site directly offshore the wall is known as Ammonias. Waves form on a shallow reef throughout the year on either an east or a south swell, but are steep and should be surfed by experts only. Kalapakī Beach, adjoining the northern end of the park, offers excellent conditions for swimmers.

Kalapakī Beach

Nawiliwili, oia ke awa kumoku. Aia ilaila ka heiau o Kuhiau. Kalapaki, aia oia makai o Nawiliwili.

Nawiliwili is the harbor. The temple of Kuhiau is there. Kalapaki is on the shoreline of Nawiliwili.

"Kaua'i Place Names"
Kelsey Collection

Kalapakī Beach is one of Kaua'i's most popular and heavily used beaches. It is the white sand beach closest to Līhu'e, one of the chief population centers of the island, and it fronts the Westin Kaua'i Resort, a major visitor destination. The ocean bottom is sandy and gently sloping, providing favorable conditions for good swimming. The surfing site known as Kalapakī offshore the beach is an ideal beginner's surfing break with gentle waves that roll across a shallow sand bar. The beach itself is a quarter of a mile long and very wide. All of these attractions draw many beachgoers from both the resident and visitor populations.

Kalapakī is one of Kaua'i's historic surfing sites. The break was surfed and bodysurfed by ancient Hawaiians and later by non-Hawaiians who took up the sports.

Kalapakī Beach was for many years the site of the Rice family's beach home. William Harrison Rice and Mary Sophia Rice came to Hawai'i as missionaries in 1841; today, many of their descendants are scattered throughout the islands. In 1870, their son William Hyde Rice purchased a large amount of land from Princess Ruth Ke'elikolani, including certain lands in Līhu'e, and the land surrounding Kalapakī Beach, where Rice built a beach home. The Rice children learned to swim, surf, and sail at Kalapakī. In later years the Kaua'i Surf Hotel

NININI. Ninini Beach is a small pocket of sand tucked into the sea cliffs outside of Nāwiliwili Harbor. In 1982 Hurricane 'Iwa decimated this area, killing many of the trees that once grew here. The lone *hala* or pandanus tree behind the beach was one of the few native trees to survive.

4

was built where the Rices' beach home had stood, and even more recently, in 1987, the Westin Kaua'i Resort opened on the site of the Kaua'i Surf Hotel.

Today the waves at Kalapakī continue to attract surfers, bodysurfers, and a large number of bodyboarders. High surf coming from an easterly or southerly direction commonly enters the harbor and breaks at the beach. During these periods of high surf, the congested mixture of bodyboarders, many of whom are younger children and inexperienced visitors, and surfers occasionally results in dangerous collisions. High surf also generates powerful rip currents in the nearshore areas.

Kalapakī is popular for many other types of ocean recreation besides surfing, bodysurfing, and bodyboarding. These include canoe surfing, fishing, snorkeling, windsurfing, and twin-hull sailing. The beach may be reached from Nāwiliwili Park at its western boundary.

Ninini Beach

Site 100. Ninini heiau, in Kalapaki near the site of the Nawiliwili light house. It is now all destroyed.

Archaeology of Kauai
Bennet, 1931

Ninini Beach is located near the northern point of Nāwiliwili Harbor. The beach actually consists of two large pockets of white sand, separated by lava rock at the base of a low sea cliff. Both of these pocket beaches, tucked into the northern side of the harbor, are normally protected from the prevailing winds and currents. However, they are subject at all times of the year to high surf and *kona* (southerly) storms, both of which may generate dangerous water conditions.

The smaller pocket beach, approximately one-quarter mile from Ninini Point, is rocky at the water's edge with pockets of sand and rock immediately offshore. Swimming and snorkeling conditions are good. A trail leads down to the beach from the road above. This secluded site is occasionally used by nudists.

The larger beach, inland of the first, is much more appealing to sunbathers and swimmers with its gentle, rock-free slope leading into a sandy ocean bottom. Snorkeling conditions are good. During periods of high surf, bodysurfers frequent the shorebreak. A trail provides access to the beach from the road above. Some residents know this site as Running Waters Beach because of irrigation runoff that was once discharged into the coastal waters from the sugar cane fields nearby.

In 1987 Amfac Hawaii Inc. sold 175 acres of fee simple land at Ninini Point and leased 208 adjoining acres to Hemmeter-VMS Kaua'i Company I, the company that developed and built the Westin Kaua'i Resort at Kalapakī Beach. The newly acquired lands included the cattle pastures and sugar cane fields above Ninini Beach.

To reach Ninini Beach, turn off Ahukini Road where it meets the ocean. Follow the Līhu'e Plantation Company dirt road south along the ocean for 2.6 miles to Ninini Point. The point is marked by the Nāwiliwili Light Station and the foundations of the former lighthouse keeper's quarters. The view from the lighthouse area is spectacular, and there is an excellent vantage point for watching the boats moving in and out of the harbor. The point is also very popular with shoreline fishermen.

Ahukini State Recreation Pier

Ahukini, oia ka inoa nui o ka 'aina a hiki Hanama'ulu.

Ahukini is the overall name of the land next to Hanama'ulu.

"Kaua'i Place Names"
Kelsey Collection

Ahukini State Recreation Pier is a small, one-acre park on the southern point of Hanamā'ulu Bay. The pier is an old landing that was formerly known as Ahukini Landing. The original site, a small-boat landing, was improved by the Ahukini Terminal Company in the early 1920s to facilitate shipping service to the plantations in the Līhu'e, Kawaihau, and Kīlauea districts. By 1924, the company had built the pier and a 300-foot-long breakwater and had dredged a turning basin. It also built and operated the railroad that ran from Ahukini to the Līhu'e Mill and from Ahukini to Keālia, via Kapa'a.

The pier at Ahukini was the first on Kaua'i at which interisland and overseas vessels could tie up for loading and unloading. It was used extensively, particularly during World War II, until 1945. During the post-war period, all shipping operations at Ahukini were relocated at Nāwiliwili Harbor, which had been improved to accommodate vessels that were too large to enter Ahukini. The facilities at Ahukini were then slowly vacated, and by June of 1950 the site was abandoned.

The pier was later dismantled, and in 1978 Ahukini Landing was converted into a park by the establishment of the Ahukini State Recreation Pier. It is a very popular fishing site, especially with pole fishermen. Spear and net fishermen should be aware that certain spearing and netting activities are prohibited from the pier and within the surrounding waters of Hanamā'ulu Bay. Details of the regulations may be obtained from the State Department of Land and Natural Resources.

Hanamā'ulu Beach Park

Hanamaulu Bay suffers from high turbidity and poor water circulation. After heavy rainfall, a turbid surface plume of freshwater, 2 to 5 feet in depth, extends onto the bay from the stream mouth. Early in this century, a groin was constructed at the bay mouth to provide calm anchorage for ships calling at the old sugar landing pier. This structure impedes water exchange with the open ocean.

"Kauai Island Coastal Resource Inventory"
AECOS, 1982

Hanamā'ulu Beach Park is located at the head of Hanamā'ulu Bay, a wide bay that is well protected from the open ocean. The park is a popular picnic and camping site for local residents. The narrow sand beach that fronts the park slopes gently into a shallow, sandy sea bottom nearshore. Although the conditions seem ideal for swimming, the bay waters are usually murky and not particularly appealing for in-water activities. Hanamā'ulu Stream crosses the southern end of the beach, discharging its silt-laden waters into the bay. The ocean currents circulating in the inner bay areas are not strong enough to flush out the murky water, so it lingers at the park's shoreline.

During the early 1970s the water flowing in Hanamā'ulu Stream was not only dirty, but polluted as well.

On June 9, 1972, the beach at Hanamā'ulu was closed for public use due to the high bacterial pollution levels in the nearshore waters and in the adjoining stream. The pollution came from fecal matter from pasture animals in the upper valley and from the piggeries in upper Kapaia. It was spread by runoff into the stream from plantation irrigation water. The beach was reopened for public swimming in June two years later when the pollution problems were corrected.

The outer reaches of Hanamā'ulu Bay are much cleaner and attract scuba divers and other fishermen. Commercial net fishermen surround *akule* and other migratory schooling fish that appear seasonally. Mullet and sharks, particularly juvenile hammerheads, are also found in the bay.

Nukoli'i Beach Park

The site has long since ceased to be a dairy, but has retained the old Nukolii Dairy's name. It is a windswept stretch of coastline adjacent to the Wailua Golf Course.

Much of the beach runs right into a shoreline reef. Shore fishermen cast their bait beyond the reef and set poles in the sand back of it. Horses are tethered inland amid low shrubs and sparse grass.

Honolulu Advertiser
October 31, 1980

For many residents of Kaua'i the name Nukoli'i was once synonymous with political strife and controversy that began in the 1970s. In 1974 a development firm purchased 60 acres of beachfront agricultural land at the site of the former Nukoli'i Dairy. Although the dairy had long since ceased its operations, the undeveloped shoreline pastures were used by local residents for fishing and other recreational activities. In 1976 the State Land Use Commission reclassified the site to urban zoning, and late in 1977 the Kaua'i General Plan was amended to include resort zoning for the parcel. These changes generated a ground swell of public concern to save what many residents considered to be the last undeveloped shoreline between Līhu'e and Kapa'a.

In 1979 the Kaua'i County Council granted resort zoning for 25 of the 60 acres and gave permission for the construction of a 350-room hotel and a 150-unit condominium complex. A citizens' group, the Committee to Save Nukoli'i, responded to the council's action by starting a drive for a referendum to reverse the zoning. By early 1980 the committee had collected 4,500 voters' signatures, a sufficient number to place the zoning question on the November 1980 ballot.

Meanwhile, the county continued to approve various permits for the development. The hotel building permit was issued the day before the election. Although the electorate voted 10,794 to 5,618 to restore the agricultural zoning, Judge Kei Hirano on February 9, 1981, ruled that the permits had been validly issued and the developers had vested rights to proceed with the project. The developers began construction.

Then in 1982, with 30 percent of the hotel and all of the condominium units completed, the Hawaii Supreme Court reversed Judge Hirano's decision and halted the project. The United States Supreme Court refused to hear an appeal from the developer. The Hawaii Supreme Court instructed Judge Hirano to issue an order halting construction and to consider solutions to the conflict.

In 1983 a group supporting the development, Kauaians for Nukoli'i, began its own petition drive to ask voters if resort status should be restored. The group, which received most of its funding from the developer, was allowed to pay the costs of a special election in February 1984 rather than wait for the general election in November.

The pre-election campaigns sharply divided the people of Kaua'i, and the battle between the developer and the Committee to Save Nukoli'i proved to be one of the most heated political issues ever seen in Hawai'i. On February 4, 1984, the voters in the special election decided in favor of resort zoning. The Committee to Save Nukoli'i challenged the election's validity in the 9th U.S. Circuit Court of Appeals, but the court upheld the legality of the proceedings.

Early in 1986 the 350-room, 60-million-dollar Kaua'i Hilton Hotel opened its doors to the public. The condominium units, known as the Kaua'i Beach Villas, are part of the complex and are operated and maintained by the hotel.

In the same year, the county completed its own development at Nukoli'i, a beach park with facilities including a comfort station, showers, and parking. Coconut trees were planted between the building and the shoreline. The beach park is located at the end of Kaua'i Hilton Road.

The Nukoli'i shoreline is bordered by a long, narrow beach fronted by beachrock. The nearshore bottom is shallow and rocky with scattered pockets of sand. Conditions are fair for swimming and good for snorkeling, diving, and pole fishing. Surfers occasionally ride a break called Graveyards. A wide fringing reef offshore offers good protection to the nearshore areas under normal trade wind conditions. The beach fronting the Wailua Golf Course between Nukoli'i and Lydgate State Park is a continuation of Nukoli'i Beach.

Lydgate State Park

A small site has been set aside at Lihue, Kauai, to be known as Lydgate Memorial Park. At its Wailua entrance a monument has been erected in which is inserted a bronze plate indicating its purpose, as above, erected by the Kauai Chamber of Commerce as a tribute to the late J. M. Lydgate, whose energy and foresight resulted in establishing the beautiful and historic spots of Kauai as public parks.

Thrum's Hawaiian Annual
1924

Lydgate State Park, located on Leho Drive, south of the Kaua'i Resort, was named for the Reverend John M. Lydgate, a once-prominant civic leader on Kaua'i and former pastor of Līhu'e Union Church and Koloa Church. He was a noted authority on Hawaiian literature, folklore, legends, and land titles. Lydgate served a term as Territorial land agent for Kaua'i, was a managing director of McBryde Sugar Company, and was the editor of the *Garden Island* newspaper for a time before his death in Līhu'e on November 28, 1922.

The park is located on the shoreline near the mouth of the Wailua River. It is one of the most popular beach parks on Kaua'i and attracts many swimmers, picnickers, campers, fishermen, surfers, divers, and beachcombers. Windsurfers also visit the area when south, or *kona,* winds offer favorable sailing conditions for this side of the island.

One of the park's major attractions is its large, dou-

LYDGATE STATE PARK. A boulder breakwater shelters the beach at Lydgate State Park, providing a safe, shallow swimming area for families with little children. Two early morning sunbathers take advantage of the deserted beach, a favorite site among local residents for swimming and picnicing.

ble-sectioned salt-water pool. The pool was constructed in 1970 by placing huge boulders in a semicircle facing the beach. The interior of the boulder breakwater is divided into one large, deep pool and one small, shallow pool. Local residents consider the sand-bottomed pools to be one of Kaua'i's safest year-round swimming sites. The breakwater offers good protection from the prevailing currents and from the seasonally high surf.

Signs posted onshore prohibit fishing from the breakwater and warn swimmers to keep off the slippery boulders, especially during periods of high surf. High surf washing over the breakwater deposits all kinds of debris in the pools, and swimmers should be especially cautious of heavy branches and logs that may roll and cause injuries.

Lydgate State Park offers a variety of facilities and can accommodate many large groups at one time.

Group picnic permits are issued at the state park's office in Līhu'e.

Wailua Beach

Wailua-kai is the sparkling region on Kauai where the sun shines almost always, and the sea responds with the roar and flash and spray of unchecked combers until they dash themselves down on Papaloa beach.

Honolulu Star-Bulletin
September 5, 1936

Wailua Beach is a popular destination for visitors and residents. The 100-foot-wide beach stretches for a half-mile between the mouth of the Wailua River and a rocky point to the north. The nearshore bottom fronting most of the beach is a shallow sand bar. Waves breaking throughout the year on the sand bar offer favorable surfing conditions for bodysurfers, bodyboarders, and surfers. During periods of high surf, however, particularly in winter and spring, dangerous water conditions often develop, especially strong rip currents. A powerful rip often runs seaward at the north end of the beach where water washing across the shallow sand bar drains into the deeper waters of Wailua Bay. Rip currents are also found in the center of the beach and at the southern end near the river.

At the southern end of the bay, Wailua River crosses the beach and meets the ocean. Wailua River is one of the few navigable rivers in the state. Daily boat tours take visitors up-river from Wailua River Marina to Fern Grotto, one of Kaua'i's most famous visitor attractions. The grotto is an amphitheater-shaped cave that provides excellent acoustics. Ferns grow upside-down from the ceiling of the cave. Tour guides traditionally sing the Hawaiian Wedding Song to their groups at the cave, and many couples have been married there.

The broad Wailua River is a popular water skiing site. The ski boats are launched from a single-lane ramp in Wailua River State Park, directly opposite the marina. The ramp is also used to launch fishing boats, jet skis, kayaks, and outrigger canoes. During most of the year, a shallow sand bar across the mouth of the river prevents most craft from traveling from the river to the ocean. The sand bar occasionally disappears for short periods of time after heavy rains in the uplands, which swell the river and wash away the sand at its mouth. The rapid erosion of the sand bar is a very spectacular event and often takes only several hours to complete.

The entire Wailua River region, including Wailua Beach, is of exceptional archaeological and historic interest. It was once a very productive agricultural area, supporting a large population. At the mouth of the river a series of Hawaiian temples *(heiau)* and other sacred sites comprise one of the most important archaeological complexes on Kaua'i. Many of the sites, identified with historical markers, can be seen in the state park. Near the river mouth, boulders with petroglyphs are exposed periodically when the sand bar is eroded.

In the northern corner of the bay, surfers ride an offshore break called Horners. The site was named for Albert Horner, a pioneer of the pineapple industry on the eastern part of Kaua'i. From 1920 to 1953 Horner was manager of Hawaiian Canneries Company, a pineapple growing and canning operation organized by his father in 1914. The company first planted pine at Kapahi and then expanded its fields to Moloa'a.

In 1929 Horner built a twenty-room mansion on a 4-acre estate inland of the surfing site. The home was a landmark at the beach until 1976 when the property was purchased by Mel and Pauline Ventura. The Venturas put up a condominium complex called Lae Nani on the beachfront property, but rather than demolish the beautiful old house, they decided to make it their family home. They hired a house-moving firm to disassemble, transport, and reassemble the 5,500-square-foot house on its present site across the road from 'Ōpaeka'a Falls in Wailua. Although the house is no longer on the shoreline, the surfing break is still known as Horners, and this northern corner of Wailua Beach is commonly called Lae Nani Beach.

Wailua Beach is directly across Kūhiō Highway from the Coco Palms Resort. There are no public facilities at the beach.

Waipouli Beach

Waipouli was a rather insignificant *ahupua'a* south of Kapa'a, watered by Konohiki Stream, in the bed of which there were flats where taro was once planted. There is some level, swampy land by the sea that looks as if it had been terraced.

Native Planters in Old Hawaii
Handy, Handy, and Pukui, 1972

Waipouli Beach is a long, narrow beach that winds along the shoreline from the Coconut Plantation Resort to Waika'ea Canal in Kapa'a. Shoreline access is interrupted about midway along the beach by Moikeha Canal. There is no pedestrian bridge spanning this small drainage canal.

The backshore of Waipouli Beach is lined with long rows of tall ironwood trees. A shoreline pedestrian trail through the trees is much used by strollers and joggers. At the water's edge, most of the beach is fronted by wide sections of beachrock. Seaward of the beachrock the nearshore bottom drops quickly to overhead depths and is subject to strong currents at all times of the year. Several patches of reef at the southern end of the beach offer some protection from the nearshore currents, but even this area should be avoided during periods of high surf, most common in the winter and spring. High surf generates dangerous rip currents along the entire length of Waipouli Beach. The marginal swimming conditions make the beach more attractive to fishermen than to swimmers.

Although most of the Waipouli shoreline is developed or privately owned, six public rights-of-way provide access to the beach. They are all marked and easy to locate.

Kapa'a Beach Park

'Auhea iho nei la 'o Makee
A ka Malulani la e huli hele nei

Aia aku nei kahi i Kapa'a
Ka waiho kapakahi i ka 'apapa

'O ke kani honehone a ke oeoe
A e ha'i mai ana la i ka lono.

Where is the Makee?
The Malulani looks everywhere.

There she is at Kapa'a
Keeled over on the reef.

Softly sounds the whistle
Telling the news.

"Hula 'o Makee"
Traditional song

The sand beach that fronts Kapa'a town and Kapa'a Beach Park has been narrowed as the result of severe shoreline erosion that began in 1959. A massive section of the shallow reef offshore Moikeha Canal was dredged, first by Līhu'e Plantation for 180,000 cubic yards of road fill, and then again by the county for a proposed natatorium. This led to the loss of sand from Kapa'a Beach because the dredged area trapped the sand that normally replenished the beach. Surveys made in June 1959 and January 1963 showed that an average of 40 feet of beach width was lost along a 1,000-foot-long section of shoreline. In 1964 the state completed a revetment in the area in an attempt to stop the erosion. Artificial structures along the shoreline today include jetties at the mouths of two drainage canals and the 900-

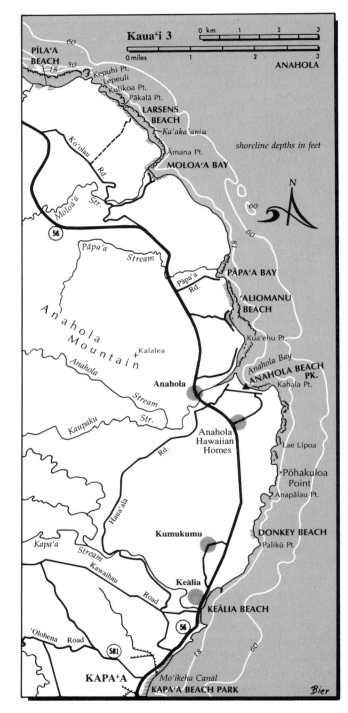

foot-long revetment at the north end of the beach park.

Off Kapa'a Beach Park the nearshore bottom is shallow and rocky. Although it is not a particularly appealing site for swimming, several large sand pockets are deep enough at high tide for swimmers. The wide, shallow reef offshore attracts many local fishermen who spear fish, hunt for octopus, and gather seaweed. The reef is one of the few places on Kaua'i where *lamalama,* or torch fishing, is still seen on moonless, low-tide nights.

The only boat ramp on the windward side of Kaua'i is located at the southern end of Kapa'a Beach Park in Waika'ea Canal. Directly offshore of the canal, a wide channel cuts through the reef to the open ocean. Lighted markers line the outer reaches of the channel.

Waika'ea Canal is one of several in Waipouli and Kapa'a that were built to drain the inland marshes to make the land suitable for agriculture. In former times both sugar cane and rice were grown here in abundance. For many years the canal has served as a landing for local boaters. In 1977 a small paved ramp was constructed on the canal's south bank, but boaters have problems with the site. During the development of Kapa'a Beach Park, a former train bridge seaward of the ramp was converted into a pedestrian bridge, which is quite low, severely limiting the size of boats able to pass under it, particularly at high tide. In spite of this limitation, the ramp is still heavily used because there is no other for miles in either direction.

Waika'ea Canal is a popular area for picknicking and fishing. Fishing restrictions in effect at the site include no multi-hook fishing and no crabbing with more than 10 nets per person. Additional information regarding restrictions on the netting of shrimp, juvenile fish, and commercial baitfish such as *nehu* and *'iao* may be obtained from the State Department of Land and Natural Resources.

Keālia Beach

I [John Rapoza] came to Kapaa November 1, 1883, on the S.S. James McKee. I was then twenty-one years of age and with my parents. The trip from Honolulu to Kapaa was made in the usual time of 15 hours, but it was far worse than the 60-day trip we made from Europe.

I was under a three-year contract to work on the plantation. We received $9 a month for our work and $8 a month for "kaukau."

Originally, the sugar from Kealia was sent to Kapaa in wagons drawn by California horses. The railroad track was made from Kealia Mill to Kapaa Landing about 1886. I drove the horses or mules on these cars. Two small locomotives were bought about 1890.

The steamer James McKee could take 2500 bags of sugar. The Kaala took 2000 bags.

The Garden Island
August 18, 1978

Keālia means "the salt bed" or "the salt-encrusted area." In former times flat, low-lying shoreline sites were periodically flooded by high surf and high tides. Shallow ponds would often form. After several days of exposure to the sun, the water that had inundated the flats would evaporate, leaving behind a thin layer or occasionally a pocket of salt. Salt from the deeper pockets was gathered to satisfy a variety of domestic, medicinal, and ceremonial needs. The name Keālia, or a form of the name, is found on all of the major Hawaiian islands, including Ni'ihau and Kaho'olawe.

Keālia was once a plantation town with a sugar mill and a train depot. An interisland steamer landing was situated at the north end of Keālia Beach. Little remains of the former town. Today, sugar cane from the surrounding fields is trucked to a mill in Līhu'e, and the bulk sugar produced by the mill is shipped out of Nāwiliwili Harbor. The only major commercial activity in Keālia today is sand-mining of the extensive dunes just inland of the highway. These are the only significant dunes left on the windward side of the island since the extensive dunes in Waipouli and Kapa'a were leveled for development.

About 150 feet wide and half a mile long, Keālia Beach lies between two rocky points. The nearshore bottom is a long sand bar whose depth constantly changes. Surf breaks on the sand bar throughout year, attracting a constant flow of bodyboarders and surfers. Most of these wave riders tend to congregate at the north end of the beach, where the best waves are usually found. High surf during the winter and spring on Kaua'i's north shore wraps around the island and breaks at Keālia. It

KEĀLIA. The inland areas of Keālia are extensively cultivated in sugar cane by Līhue Plantation Company. Keālia Stream cuts across the south end of Keālia Beach, depositing cane trash on the sand. Surfing and bodyboarding are popular in the shorebreak at the opposite end of the beach, the site of the former Keālia Landing.

often undermines the sand bar, exposing the bedrock below. During these periods of high surf, nearshore rip currents are very powerful and dangerous. Over the years many drownings and near-drownings have occurred here. At the north end of the beach, a small jetty offers swimmers some protection from the surf. The jetty is all that remains of the former Keālia Landing.

The beach is easily accessible from Kūhiō Highway. Beachgoers unfamiliar with the area should be aware that they must cross a cane-haul road parallel to the highway in the rear of the beach. Heavy trucks laden with sugar cane use the road whenever fields are being harvested to the north of Keālia.

Donkey Beach

When [the plantation] is preparing a field for a ratoon crop (cane growing from the roots or stumps of cane),

the burros (or donkeys) come out of their pasture and are fitted with special back packs. These packs enable the burros to carry about 250 pounds of seed cane, carefully cut into average sized lengths, into the fields.

The burros are able to climb over flumes and cross difficult terrain which would be impossible for machines to manuever. The bundles of seed cane are dropped in strategic locations in the fields, where workmen plant them in the "blank" spaces between the regular ratoon crop.

The burros are used about eight or nine months of the year. The rest of the time, they relax in their pasture.

Honolulu Advertiser
May 27, 1966

Although modern vehicles and machinery have long since replaced donkeys, horses, and mules as work animals on the sugar plantations, mules are still used occasionally for certain types of jobs. One of these jobs is

DONKEY BEACH. A lone swimmer contemplates the storm surf conditions on a cold, windy day at Donkey Beach. Līhue Plantation Company once kept large herds of donkeys and mules in the pastures behind the beach, giving the site its popular name. Palikū Point is the promontory lined with ironwood trees at the far end of the beach.

hauling bundles of seed cane and bags of fertilizer into the fields. The bundles and bags are brought to the fields by trucks and are then hauled through the planted fields by the animals. Plantation workers plant the seed cane and scatter the fertilizer by hand.

For many years Līhu‘e Plantation Company kept a large herd of mules and donkeys in the pasture behind the beach at Palikū. For this reason the beach was named Donkey Beach. When nearby Keālia was in full swing as a plantation town, many of the animals grazed in the shoreline pastures, but today only a few mules remain.

Donkey Beach, located 1.5 miles from Keālia Beach, is a large, picturesque pocket of sand north of Palikū Point at the base of a rocky, sloping pasture filled with ‘ilima, naupaka, ironwoods, and a large grove of hau. The backshore is lined with beach heliotrope. The steep foreshore indicates the force of the high surf that sea-sonally sweeps the beach. A surfing site immediately offshore is popular with surfers, bodyboarders, and bodysurfers. The waves form over a flat, rocky bottom. During the winter and spring, high surf creates danger-ous ocean conditions, including a pounding shorebreak, strong backwashes, and powerful rip currents. A num-ber of drownings and many near-drownings have oc-curred here.

Donkey Beach is not visible from Kūhiō Highway, and there are no public rights-of-way to it. Līhu‘e Plan-tation Company has erected gates and posted no tres-passing signs on all of its roads leading to the beach. The wide dirt road that parallels the beach is a major cane-haul thoroughfare that is heavily used by large trucks; it is a one-way road heading toward Keālia. Out of its concern to avoid traffic accidents between the public's vehicles and the cane-haul trucks, the planta-tion has prohibited public access to the site.

In spite of the restricted access, surfers and other beachgoers still manage to find their way to Donkey Beach. Its isolation makes it one of the most popular sites on Kaua'i for nude sunbathers, who should be aware, however, that nudity on public beaches is not legal in Hawai'i.

The shoreline between Donkey Beach and Anahola Beach Park consists of 2 miles of low sea cliffs. Interspersed among the cliffs are a number of small bays and coves, at least four of which contain small pockets of sand. Although the bays and coves have rocky bottoms which deter recreational swimming, they are popular sites for pole fishing, diving, throw-netting, and beachcombing. This rocky shoreline collects large amounts of windblown debris; it is a favorite site for beachcombers eager to find the hand-blown glass Japanese longline fishing floats known locally as glass balls.

Immediately north of Donkey Beach is a surfing site called 14 Crack. A deep crevice or "crack" in the reef once harbored a wide variety of reef fish, making it a popular place for throw-netting and diving. Old-time fishermen who frequented the site named it 14 Crack for Līhu'e Sugar Plantation's Field 14 immediately inland. In recent years the name has occasionally been reversed to Crack 14. The surfing break is an excellent left that works best on an easterly winter swell.

Anahola Beach Park is located in the lee of Kahala Point in the south corner of Anahola Bay. This narrow little park is much used by neighborhood residents, especially during the summer months. Offshore, a shallow reef flat extends from Kahala Point to the ruins of the old landing on Anahola Beach which was constructed in 1900. The reef protects the park's shoreline and several nearshore pockets of sand from high surf. Local residents consider this spot one of the safest year-round swimming areas for children on the windward side of the island. A surfing break is located at the outer edge of the reef, but board surfing is prohibited to ensure the safety of non-surfers.

Anahola Beach adjoins the north end of the beach park. A sand bar fronts most of this very long, wide beach. The shorebreak that forms on the sand bar attracts bodysurfers, bodyboarders, and surfers. Surfers also ride a break called Unreals next to the old landing. The beach is popular with pole fishermen, and especially with beachcombers who come from all over the island to hunt for Japanese longline fishing floats or "glass balls." During the winter and spring, high surf generates dangerous ocean conditions, including a pounding shorebreak and powerful rip currents. Anahola Stream at the north end of the beach is often barred by sand during dry weather.

Anahola Beach Park

Hanohano Kalalea kau mai iluna
O ka pali kaulana a o Anahola.

I laila ho'i au i ka iho 'aina
Nā ke kaula likini mōliolio.

Huli aku nānā 'ia Amu
I ka makani alo 'ehu hele uluulu.

Glorious Kalalea that stands above
The famous cliff of Anahola.

It is there that I descend
The rope taut as rigging.

I turn and look at Amu
The elusive wind that stirs up seaspray.

"Anahola"
Traditional song

'Aliomanu Beach

Of all the aquatic activities that occur at the 'Aliomanu Reef, the most widely known is the harvesting of limu kohu, the seaweed *Asparagopsis taxiformis*. Although this limu is found on O'ahu and the Big Island, as well as Kaua'i, the Anahola District is one of the most famous places for its collection for both home consumption and commercial distribution.

"Kaua'i Island Coastal Resources Inventory"
AECOS, 1982

'Aliomanu Beach begins at the north end of Anahola Beach and ends at the sea cliffs which border Pāpa'a Bay. It is a narrow sand beach with a nearshore bottom that is shallow and rocky, precluding swimming in most places. Several public rights-of-way lead to the beach, and fishermen camp in a number of small clearings in the backshore. Beyond Kuaʻehu Point, ʻAliomanu Road is washed out and impassable by automobile.

The major attraction at ʻAliomanu is not the beach but the extensive reef offshore, one of the longest and widest fringing reefs on Kauaʻi. The reef is widely used for a number of commercial and recreational activities, including pole fishing, throw-netting, gill netting, spearfishing, octopus spearing, torch fishing, and seaweed harvesting. It is most famous as a good place for harvesting *limu kohu,* an edible seaweed.

This seaweed, *Asparagopsis taxiformis* to the botanists, is found elsewhere in Hawaiʻi, but local consumers unanimously agree that the best *limu kohu* comes from Kauaʻi. Other popular harvesting reefs are Kaʻakaʻaniu and Pīlaʻa. Commercial harvesting on these reefs has for generations been the domain of a few well-known Hawaiian families from Anahola and Moloaʻa, the two communities closest to the reefs. These families have always observed conservation practices in their harvesting methods to insure the future availability of the supply. Only the upper sections of the plants are removed, leaving the base or "roots" to grow new stems. This practice, coupled with the high surf and rough ocean conditions that prevail most of the year on these reefs, have protected this important native resource.

PĀPAʻA. Pāpaʻa Bay is a small, isolated bay in the lee of the high sea cliff northwest of Anahola. During periods of high surf strong rip currents run seaward along the bay's rocky southeastern margin. The white-water trail below the rocks indicates that lesser rip currents also form during periods of low surf.

The plants are commonly found growing along the seaward edge of the reef where there is a constant flow of water from breaking waves. In the water they resemble a forest of tiny pink pine trees. The Hawaiians make a distinction between *limu kohu lipehe,* a milder flavored, light red variety, and *limu kohu koko,* a stronger flavored, dark red variety.

Limu kohu remains one of the most sought after and highly priced seaweeds in Hawai'i. After it is harvested and cleaned, the seaweed is soaked overnight in fresh water to reduce its bitter iodine flavor, drained, and lightly salted. If it is to be shipped to neighbor island markets, it is rolled into tight balls.

Pāpa'a Bay

Coral cover is moderately high (10 to 25%) in Papa'a Bay. The soft coral, *Palythoa sp.,* is common on the upper surfaces of volcanic boulders, along with the stony corals, *Pocillopora meandrina, Pirites lobaba,* and *Montipora patula.* Most of the algae are coralline forms, of which *Porolithon onkodes* is the most abundant. Fleshy algae are less common, possibly because of heavy grazing by reef fishes. Surgeonfishes, parrotfishes, and wrasses are the most abundant of the 20 to 50 fish species inhabiting the bay.

"Kaua'i Island Coastal Resources Inventory"
AECOS, 1982

Pāpa'a Bay is a small, isolated bay indenting the high sea cliff northwest of Anahola. A picturesque crescent sand beach lies at the head of the bay. A wide, sand-bottomed channel deep enough to accommodate boats runs through the center of the bay and merges with the nearshore waters at the beach. A wide, shallow reef fringes the northwest side of the channel and a smaller section of reef lines the southeast edge of the channel below the sea cliff. The nearshore waters fronting the beach offer excellent opportunities for swimming and snorkeling. During periods of high surf, waves break completely across the outer bay. A strong rip current forms inshore and runs seaward through the channel on the southeast margin of the bay.

A breeding colony of wedgetailed shearwaters is located in the low cliffs above the northwest side of the bay. The colony is monitored regularly by the refuge manager at Kīlauea Point National Wildlife Refuge.

A public road, Pāpa'a Road, leads from Kūhiō Highway to the top of the sea cliff above the bay, but there are no public rights-of-way down to the beach.

Moloa'a Bay

In passing Moloa'a, Keahi pointed to some low hills *mauka* and *makai* of the highway and said, "When I was a small girl, I used to come here with my *tutu-wahine* for *wauke.* These hills, now barren, were once so thickly overgrown that the *a'a* (roots) of the *wauke* were *molo* (matted) together, weaving into each other like the meshes of a mat. . . . This was once a great *wauke* growing place . . . Molo-a'a, Matted-roots."

Native Planters in Old Hawaii
Handy, Handy, and Pukui, 1972

The small clusters of lower-valley and shoreline homes at Moloa'a today give no indication that the area was once a large, thriving community. Shortly before the turn of the century sugar cane growing operations were established on lands surrounding the valley. The population in the area expanded tremendously with the influx of plantation workers, with the construction of a pineapple cannery, and with the establishment of many independent farms.

One of the best indicators of early population trends in the area was Ko'olau School. The one-room school opened in 1898 near the graveyard on Ko'olau Road. It eventually expanded to four rooms to accommodate the ever-increasing numbers of school-aged children. After 62 years, the growth cycle reversed itself, and in June 1960 the little school closed because the cost of maintaining a four-room school for a handful of students was too high. Today the school building is gone, and little else remains except the graveyards to indicate the size of the former community.

The beach at Moloa'a is a wide crescent of sand that curves for a quarter-mile along the shore of Moloa'a Bay. Both ends of the beach terminate at high bluffs. Beachrock fronts the west end of the beach where Moloa'a Stream meets the ocean. Windblown debris accumulates in this corner of the bay, a good place for beachcombing. High surf, particularly during the winter and spring, generates dangerous ocean conditions, including a pounding shorebreak and a powerful rip current. The rip current usually runs from the east side of the beach, along the shorebreak, and then out the center of the bay. Over the years, the rip has caused many drownings and near-drownings. During periods of calm seas, swimming, snorkeling, and diving are excellent throughout the inner bay.

Larsens Beach

L. David Larsen, vice president of C. Brewer and Co., Ltd., died Saturday at 9:10 pm of a stroke while visiting friends in Waimanalo. He was born at Stockholm, Sweden, Sept. 18, 1886 and was in his 58th year.

Mr. Larsen came to Hawaii in 1908 as a plant pathologist with the Hawaii Sugar Planters Association experiment station. In 1918 he became manager of Kilauea Sugar Plantation on Kauai, and in 1930 was appointed assistant vice president of C. Brewer and Co., Ltd. In 1932 he was vice president and director with special supervision over operations of plantations and ranches.

Honolulu Advertiser
April 10, 1944

LARSENS BEACH. The long, wide fringing reef offshore Larsens Beach is one of Hawai'i's most famous sites for seaweed gathering. Generations of Hawaiian families from nearby communities have traditionally picked *limu kohu (Asparagopsis taxiformis)* from the reef margin where the seaweed is most plentiful. Some of the seaweed is kept for home consumption, but the majority of the highly prized product is sold to local and neighbor island markets.

L. David Larsen, a former manager of Kīlauea Plantation, had a beautiful beach home for many years behind the beach that still carries his name. Larsens Beach is a long, narrow ribbon of sand that winds between Amana and Kulikoa points. The beach sits at the base of a series of low hills, most of which are used as cattle pastures. The backshore is covered by vegetation—beach heliotrope, *naupaka,* false *kamani,* and *pōhuehue.* A wide assortment of debris, such as bottles, glass balls, and shells, litters the entire beach and attracts many beachcombers.

Swimming conditions are marginal because the nearshore bottom is shallow and rocky, with only an occasional pocket of sand. Outcrops of beachrock at the water's edge are common. Pākala Point, a low rocky projection in the center of the beach, is directly inshore of a narrow channel through the reef. This is Pākala Channel, one of the major passages in the reef for water draining seaward from the shallow nearshore reef flats into the open ocean. During any period of high surf, particularly during the winter and spring, a powerful rip current runs through the channel. Over the years, the rip has caused many drownings and near-drownings.

Offshore of Larsens Beach is a very long and shallow reef, Ka'aka'aniu, which is one of Hawai'i's best known harvesting sites for the seaweed *limu kohu, Asparagopsis taxiformis.* Although *limu kohu* is harvested in other well-known areas of Kaua'i such as 'Aliomanu and Pīla'a and on other islands in the state, the reef at Ka'aka'aniu is said to grow the highest quality plants, the *limu kohu koko,* a deep red variety.

Harvesting ideally takes place on low-tide days when the reef is emergent and the seaweed is easily accessible. *Limu kohu* grows at the outer edge of the reef where the waves break, so the ocean must be calm enough to permit safe harvesting. However, if the ocean is too calm and there are no waves to play over the seaweed, it burns and turns white from exposure to the sun.

Harvesters break the individual plants off above the base, or *kumu,* from which the plants regenerate. Taking only the tops of the plants also simplifies the cleaning process. Harvesters wear cloth bags around their waists into which they place the seaweed as they move expertly along the outer margins of the reef. As it accumulates in the waist bags, the seaweed is periodically transferred into larger storage bags that are left submerged in shallow, current-free pockets in the reef. The low hills inland of Ka'aka'aniu offer an excellent vantage point from which to watch the harvesting activity. The entire reef is also a popular throw-netting site.

A public right-of-way to Larsens Beach was purchased by the county and opened in 1979. The property owner, concerned lest easy access would attract too many people to the area, agreed to sell only if the access road to the shoreline was not extended completely down to the beach. It ends, therefore, on the top of a hill, and a trail leads down to the beach. The access road meets Ko'olau Road 1.2 miles from the north intersection of Ko'olau Road and Kūhiō Highway.

Between Larsens Beach and Kepuhi Point the shoreline is primarily rocky. One small pocket of sand fronts the rocks at Lepeuli on the east side of the point. A narrow, meandering stream crosses this beach, which is frequented primarily by pole fishermen. A colony of wedgetailed shearwaters is located at Kepuhi Point.

Pīla'a Beach

Next is Pīla'a, with several small terraced areas watered by its main stream and by small streams originating in springs. This small *ahupua'a* was famous for its great old *kukui* grove. There is a small remnant of it still there. Its name was Kaukake. It was a place where the *ali'i* of Kauai met in council. There was a *heiau* in the grove. Since the *kukui* was a form of Kamapua'a we infer that the *heiau* and grove were sacred to Lono.

Native Planters in Old Hawaii
Handy, Handy, and Pukui, 1972

The *ahupua'a,* or land division, of Pīla'a runs from the mountains to the ocean and includes 2,882 acres of land. The vast tract is owned by the Mary N. Lucas Trust and has been in the Lucas family since the early 1900s. In addition to its use as a retreat by family members, portions of the property have been variously operated as a cattle ranch, a papaya farm, an alfalfa farm, and a prawn farm. In recent years the property has been managed by co-trustee and Honolulu businessman James Pflueger, one of Mary Lucas' grandsons. His name is commonly associated with Pīla'a.

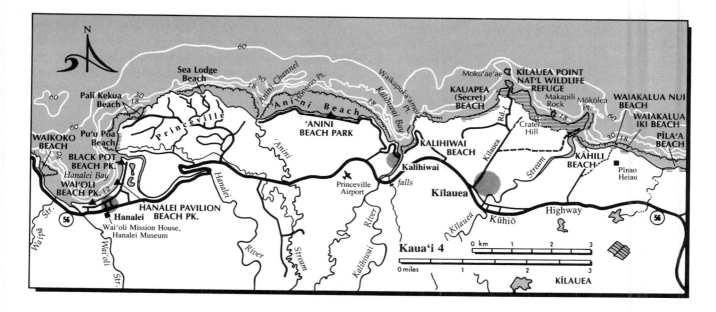

Pīla'a Beach is made up of two sections of sand divided by a low, rocky point. A small coconut grove shades several beach homes along the backshore in the eastern section. These homes, in the lee of Kepuhi Point, are situated at the base of a low, *hau*-covered bluff. A spring emanating from backshore of the bluff provides fresh water for the beach homes. The near-shore bottom is shallow and rocky with scattered pockets of sand. Swimming is primarily a high-tide activity.

A long, wide reef flat extends from Kepuhi Point all the way north to Kāhili Beach. The east section of the reef fronting Pīla'a is one of Kaua'i's famous *limu kohu* harvesting sites. The popular seaweed is also harvested from neighboring reefs at 'Aliomanu and Ka'aka'aniu. Other activities that occur along the reef at Pīla'a include surfing, throw-netting, and spearfishing.

The rocky point that separates the two sections of beach was once used by Hawaiian fishermen as a fish spotting site. One method of fishing here that involved a spotter was called *kāpeku,* or drive-netting. Many of the schooling fish that frequent Hawaiian reefs have established feeding patterns. They usually travel from one "house" *(hale)* or feeding site to another over the same "roads" *(ala).* When the tide goes out, they move into the deeper offshore waters. When the tide returns, they move back into the shallow nearshore reef flats. Taking advantage of this knowledge, native fishermen would wait for an incoming tide and simply set their nets across the "roads." A spotter on the hill watched for the fish. When the school was in position, he signaled to several men waiting quietly in the water near the "road." The men would swim up behind the fish and *kāpeku,* or kick hard, with their feet, splashing loudly and creating a commotion. The startled fish would bolt ahead down the "road" and run into the net.

The western section of Pīla'a Beach is a large, wide pocket of sand that is crossed on its western end by a small stream. The backshore is lined with coconuts, beach heliotrope, and false *kamani.* Two sand-bottomed channels separated by a patch of reef offer excellent swimming conditions. About midway to the outer edge of the reef the two small channels merge into a larger one. This channel, Pīla'a Channel, is the major drainage point in the reef for water flowing seaward from the shallow nearshore reef flats into the open ocean. During any period of high surf, particularly during winter and spring, a very powerful rip current runs through the channel. Over the years the rip has caused a number of drownings and near-drownings. During periods of high surf, swimmers who venture away from

19

shore are usually caught immediately in the seaward rush of water through the outer channel. The rolling hills at the shoreline in this area offer many excellent vantage points from which to watch the high surf and the rip current in Pīla'a Channel.

There is no direct public access to Pīla'a Beach. It can be reached by following a shoreline trail from the public right-of-way to the beach at Waiakalua Iki.

A boulder beach separates Pīla'a Beach from Waiakalua Iki Beach to the west. Immediately offshore is an extensive, lagoon-like area of coral heads and small patch reefs. During periods of calm seas, this area offers excellent opportunities for snorkeling and spearfishing.

Waiakalua Iki Beach

Another ancient heiau discovery is reported this last year from Kauai, by courtesy of Manager J. R. Myers of the

WAIAKALUA IKI. An albatross from nearby Kīlauea Point National Wildlife Refuge hovers over Waiakalua Iki Beach. Albatross have successfully nested at the refuge since 1979 and are commonly seen from Kepuhi Point (in the distance) to Princeville. Hawaiians called these birds *moli*.

Kilauea Sugar Company. It is situated on the crest of a hill or bluff overlooking the ocean, at about 1000 feet elevation, known as Waiakalua, a little to the eastward of the plantation landing. Whether this same name applies also to the temple is not quite clear.

Thrum's Hawaiian Annual
1912

Waiakalua Iki Beach is a large pocket of sand situated at the base of a small, picturesque valley. The valley borders on the coastal boundary of the Kīlauea Farms subdivision. The public right-of-way to the beach begins in the subdivision near the end of North Waiakalua Road, crosses the farm lots for 0.2 mile, and then follows a public pedestrian easement to the shoreline.

A stream crosses the west end of the beach, where the nearshore bottom is shallow and rocky. The nearshore bottom at the south end of the beach is deep enough for swimming, but is safe only during periods of calm seas. During periods of high surf a powerful rip current runs seaward through a channel in the reef directly offshore this end of the beach. Like Pīla'a Beach to the east and Waiakalua Nui Beach to the west, this isolated site is popular with fishermen and beachcombers.

At the head of the valley a small waterfall drops down the valley wall. A trail past the waterfall leads to the Kapinao *heiau* complex, the site of a pre-contact Hawaiian temple and other ruins of archaeological importance.

Waiakalua Nui Beach

There are two very small ahupua'a east of Kahili, Waiakalua-iki and Waiakalua-nui, where terrace areas were watered from several streams that originate in springs.

Native Planters in Old Hawaii
Handy, Handy, and Pukui, 1972

Waiakalua Nui Beach is almost the identical twin of Waiakalua Iki Beach to the east. It is a large pocket of sand situated at the base of a narrow but deep valley. The sand extends inland more than 100 yards. An intermittent stream channel crosses the valley floor, terminating along the backshore. The streambed is normally dry. The entire beach is fronted by beachrock. The nearshore bottom is shallow and rocky, providing very marginal swimming conditions. However, the area is popular with fishermen, sunbathers, and beachcombers. The long, wide fringing reef that begins at Kepuhi Point terminates at the north end of Waiakalua Nui Beach.

Kāhili Beach

The Honolulu District Engineer, Army Corps of Engineers, issued a federal permit on December 14 to Grove Farm Company of Lihue, Kauai, authorizing the rock revetment which had been constructed along the Kilauea Bay shoreline of the company's Kahili Quarry.

The Kahili Quarry has been in continuous use since early 1900, and the 400-foot long shoreline revetment was constructed in 1970–71 to protect the quarry crushing equipment from high tides and heavy seas.

The Garden Island
December 22, 1976

Kāhili, the "feather standard," is the name of a former interisland steamer landing, an abandoned rock quarry, and a beach. All of these sites are located in Kīlauea Bay at the mouth of Kīlauea Stream. Kāhili Beach is a long crescent of sand that is bisected by a low, rocky point. *Naupaka, hala,* false *kamani,* and ironwoods grow in the sand dunes to the rear of the beach. The dunes extend inland to the base of a series of high, heavily vegetated cliffs.

The eastern section of the beach terminates at a high, rocky point. A wide, very shallow reef flat fronting this section of the beach is a popular throw-netting site. A series of shallow patch reefs parallels the western end of the beach. The surf that breaks on these reefs is often suitable for riding. Rock Quarry, the most popular surfing site, is located directly offshore Kīlauea Stream, close to the abandoned quarry. Surfers often come here when extremely high surf closes out the rest of the north shore's surfing sites. Nearby Mōkōlea Point seems to diffuse the power of even the biggest waves; by the time the waves wrap around the point and break fronting the quarry, they have been considerably reduced in size.

The ocean bottom slopes quickly off the beach to

overhead depths. High surf, particularly during the winter and spring, generates dangerous ocean conditions, including powerful nearshore rip currents. Rips can often be seen flowing out to sea near the center of the beach and along the point fronting the river mouth. Swimmers use the beach during periods of calm seas, and pole fishermen and beachcombers are frequent visitors.

Along the backshore, the lower reaches of Kīlauea Stream form one of the most pristine estuaries in the state. In former times, it supported an important mullet fishery. Mullet and other fish are still found there, but are not fished commercially.

A long, rutted dirt road leads 1.5 miles down to Kāhili Beach from Kīlauea Road, the main road to the lighthouse. This beach access road, a public right-of-way, turns off from Kīlauea Road approximately one mile from Kūhiō Highway.

Kīlauea Point National Wildlife Refuge

A consensus having been firmly established, the Secretary of the Department of Commerce and Labor issued a terse telegraphic approval May 29, 1912 to the Bureau of Light-Houses office in San Francisco:

Concur in recommendation Hawaiian District officers . . . that light be located Kilauea Point. In good weather some masters use route north of Kauai . . . in bad weather majority masters favor light north side Kauai and best landfall.

KĪLAUEA POINT NATIONAL WILDLIFE REFUGE. Two isolated sand beaches are found at the base of Crater Hill between Mōkōlea and Kīlauea points. The smaller beach between Makapili Rock and the seacliff is a tombolo, a sandbar that connects the shoreline to an island, and is probably the best example of one in the eight major Hawaiian islands.

Ka Lae o Kilauea had undergone a landmark decision as to its future; formal construction on the site began in July 1912.

Kilauea Point Lighthouse
Aikin, 1988

Kīlauea Point National Wildlife Refuge is one of the most spectacular sections of shoreline in the Hawaiian Islands. The refuge encompasses 160 acres of exceptionally beautiful and rugged sea cliffs that include Mōkōlea Point, Crater Hill, and Kīlauea Point. The area harbors at least seven species of seabirds: wedge-tailed shearwaters, red-footed boobies, brown boobies, Laysan albatrosses, red-tailed and white-tailed tropic birds, and great frigate birds. The refuge is one of the few places in the world where the public can view the nesting colonies of central Pacific seabirds.

The high sea cliffs offer an excellent vantage point for watching Hawai'i's high surf during the winter and spring months and to observe other marine life, such as whales, dolphins, seals, and turtles. The vegetation in the area consists almost entirely of native coastal plants, thanks to efforts of the refuge staff and volunteers who remove introduced vegetation and replace it with native plants. The three contiguous parts of the refuge, Mōkōlea Point, Crater Hill, and Kīlauea Point, back a bay approximately one mile wide.

Kīlauea Point is the northernmost site on Kaua'i. This section of coastline includes several unique geological features. Crater Hill is the remnant of a tuff cone, a cone that formed from the consolidation or natural cementing of volcanic ash. Tuff cones such as Punchbowl and Diamond Head are common on O'ahu, but Crater Hill is the only example on Kaua'i. At the base of the eroded cone is Makapili Rock, a small islet perforated by a sea arch. A sand bar joins Makapili Rock to the island. This bridging sand bar is called a tombolo, and is one of only a few examples in Hawai'i. Nearby, there is also a small, isolated pocket beach at the base of Crater Hill. The best views of Crater Hill and Makapili Rock are from Mōkōlea Point. Off Kīlauea Point is a small island, Moku'ae'ae, a state seabird sanctuary, that provides an important nesting site.

The refuge at Kīlauea is part of the National Wildlife Refuge System, a unique collection of over 500 land and water areas that are managed by the U.S. Fish and Wildlife Service. In 1903 Pelican Island in Florida became the first acquisition in the system when President Theodore Roosevelt signed an executive order to protect the island's birds and designated the island as a national refuge.

Kīlauea Point National Wildlife Refuge was established in 1974 when the U.S. Fish and Wildlife Service took over a 31-acre Coast Guard reservation at Kīlauea Point. The Coast Guard had maintained the facility to service Kīlauea Lighthouse. Its light was once one of the most important in the mid-Pacific. For many years Kīlauea's beacon served as the principal landfall light for ships passing through the Hawaiian Archipelago from the Orient to mainland ports. In 1976, the 52-foot concrete lighthouse was deactivated and replaced by a 14-foot tower that stands seaward of the lighthouse.

The remaining lands in the refuge, 91 acres at Crater Hill and 38 acres at Mōkōlea Point, were acquired in 1988. Prior to their acquisition, these lands, containing important seabird nesting sites, were privately owned. The Crater Hill lands were donated to the federal government by the Doran Schmidt family, and the Mōkōlea Point lands were purchased from Oceanic Vistas Consortium for $1.6 million. The land transfers marked the conclusion of a hard-fought community campaign to protect these lands from development. The efforts of the Kīlauea Neighborhood Association–Crater Hill Coalition were successful owing largely to the intervention of the Trust for Public Lands and several key Hawaiian members of Congress. A transfer of deed ceremony was held on Crater Hill on March 8, 1988, with Representative Daniel Akaka and Senator Daniel Inouye serving as the keynote speakers.

Kīlauea Point National Wildlife Refuge is located at the end of Kīlauea Road. The turnoff from Kūhiō Highway is marked with a large sign reading "Kīlauea Lighthouse." Amenities at the refuge include a visitors' center, a book store, restrooms, and a parking area. An admission fee is charged.

Kauapea Beach

Kauapea Beach, a 3,000-foot-long, 75-foot-wide sandy beach between Kalihiwai Bay and Kilauea Point is the last long sandy beach on the north shore. This beach is only marginally accessible as it fronts on rugged, undeveloped land.

"Hawaii Regional Inventory of the National Shoreline Study"
Corps of Engineers, 1971

Kauapea Beach fronts the sea cliffs west of Kīlauea Point. It is not visible from Kūhiō Highway or any other road, and the public rights-of-way to it are unmarked. For many years its location was known only to local residents. For these reasons it was named and is still popularly known as Secret Beach.

Kauapea Beach was not "discovered" until the 1970s. Its isolated location made it particularly popular with nudists, and it soon became one of Kaua'i's most popular nudist beaches, a distinction for which it is still well known. Nudists visiting the beach should be aware that nudity on public beaches is illegal in Hawai'i. Activities in addition to sunbathing include pole fishing, surfing, bodysurfing, bodyboarding, and beachcombing.

Kauapea Beach has been the site of many drownings and near-drownings. The high surf of winter and spring months often causes dangerous water conditions, including a pounding shorebreak and very powerful rip currents. During the summer months, the ocean is usually much calmer and the beach is an excellent place for most in-water activities.

The main public right-of-way to this long, wide sand beach is an unmarked dirt road that intersects Kūhiō Highway 0.4 mile west of Kīlauea town. A trail leads to the beach from the end of the dirt road.

Kalihiwai Beach

Just outside of Kilauea is the beautiful Kalihiwai valley, whose fertile lands are watered by the river of the same name. A short sail up the river, whose banks are shaded by large trees, a beautiful little cascade is disclosed, while further inland is another and still another, which though smaller, vie in beauty with many larger waterfalls.

Tourist's Guide Through Hawaii
Whitney, 1890

Kalihiwai Beach is a wide, curving pocket of sand situated at the head of Kalihiwai Bay. It is somewhat wider at its western end where Kalihiwai River meets the ocean, and narrower at the eastern end where it abuts a boulder beach at the base of a sea cliff. A shallow, submerged rock shelf extending from the cliff provides one of the north shore's most popular surfing breaks, called simply Kalihiwai.

The surfing breaks are best here during periods of high surf in winter and spring. Surfers wait for waves at Kapuka'amoi Point, the eastern point of the bay, and ride toward shore perilously close to the towering sea cliff. Big northwest swells bring very steep and fast-breaking waves which many surfers consider some of the best on Kaua'i.

The reputation of Kalihiwai's surf attracts many residents and visitors to the area. Although the waves below the cliff are only for expert surfers, bodysurfers and bodyboarders ride waves in front of the beach proper, made possible by a wide, shallow sand bar. Surfers also ride a left-slide break that forms at the point off the stream's mouth. During periods of high surf water conditions are dangerous, particularly a pounding shorebreak, a strong backwash, and powerful rip currents. The strongest rip current commonly runs from the eastern side of the beach into the deeper bay waters. Smaller rips form throughout the shorebreak, particularly near the mouth of the stream.

During the calmer summer months, Kalihiwai is a popular boat and shoreline fishing area. It is one of the traditional sites for surround-netting of *akule*, or big-eyed scad, a popular pelagic schooling fish that frequents large, sand-bottomed bays.

A large grove of ironwoods stands in the backshore; beachgoers park their cars beneath the trees. The turnoff to the beach is west of Kīlauea at the first intersection of Kalihiwai Road and Kūhiō Highway.

'Anini Beach Park

From Anini (Wanini) at the seashore there are two stones, Pohaku Aweoweo and Pohaku 'U'u, by the sand for fishing.

"Kaua'i Place Names"
Kelsey Collection

'Anini Reef begins at Kalihiwai Bay and ends at the high sea cliffs at Princeville. One of the longest and widest fringing reefs in the Hawaiian Islands, it follows the

KALIHIWAI. The shorebreak waves at Kalihiwai Beach form throughout the year on a shallow sandbar, providing a popular site for surfers, bodyboarders, and bodysurfers. During the winter surf season expert surfers also ride the dangerous waves that roll in along the rocky base of Kapuka'amoi Point in the distance. The access road to the beach cuts through the vegetation above the point.

shoreline for 2 miles and at its widest point extends 1,600 feet offshore. The nearshore areas along 'Anini Beach are shallow, but the ocean bottom slopes to overhead depths midway to the outer edge of the reef. The outer reef edge is shallow again and often emergent during low tides.

'Anini Channel, a large, sand-bottomed gap, bisects the reef to the west of the beach park. During periods of calm seas, this channel attracts windsurfers, snorkelers, spear fishermen, and boaters. A good area for scuba diving is along the channel's outer margins, where it reaches depths of 60 feet. The channel provides drainage through the reef for water that flows from the shallow nearshore reef flats into the open ocean. During periods of high surf, the rip current that flows through the channel is extremely dangerous. Over the years, a number of drownings and near-drownings have occurred here.

'Anini Reef offers excellent opportunities for many recreational activities: spearing octopus and fish, throw-net fishing, gill-net fishing, torch fishing, seaweed harvesting, reef walking, snorkeling, windsurfing, beachcombing, and boating. The center for these activities is 'Anini Beach Park located midway along the beach, although good snorkeling is also found north of 'Anini Channel. Facilities in the park are provided for picnickers and campers. A boat ramp accommodates smaller, shallow-draft trailered boats. During the 1980s, windsurfing at 'Anini Beach Park became one of the area's most popular activities. The site is particularly good for beginners.

'Anini Beach is known to many older residents as Wanini Beach. Apparently, the name was inadvertently altered when the *W* on a park or street sign was either obscured or left out, leaving it 'Anini.

Princeville

Princeville Plantation is located on the banks of this beautiful river (Hanalei), and has the reputation of having the best sugar mill and plant in the group. Certain it is that a large fortune was expended by its former proprietor, Mr. R. C. Wyllie, in developing the productive capacity of this valley. Since his death in 1865, the estate has passed into other hands, and is now managed by Capt. John G. Ross, who is also part owner. With a fine mill and extensive tracts of the richest bottom as well as upland, this estate must become, when the system of irrigation is introduced, one of the most productive and valuable on our islands.

Hawaiian Guide Book
Whitney, 1875

Mirage Princeville Resort is a combination resort and residential community. Part of what was once a 10,000-acre cattle ranch, Princeville occupies 2,000 acres along the sea cliffs between 'Anini Beach and Hanalei Bay. The complex is made up of condominium units, single-family homes, the Sheraton Princeville Hotel, and a championship golf course.

The name Princeville originated with a former owner of the area, Robert Wyllie (1798–1865), a Scottish physician. Wyllie served the Kingdom of Hawaii as foreign minister under Kamehamehas IV and V. He held the position from 1845 until his death twenty years later. During the 1850s, he purchased a coffee plantation in the Hanalei District and replanted its lands with sugar. When, in 1860, Kamehameha IV and Queen Emma visited Wyllie's plantation with their two-year-old son, the prince Ka Haku o Hawai'i, Wyllie, in a traditional Hawaiian gesture, named his estate Princeville in honor of this visit.

In later years, this beautiful area became a cattle ranch, and in 1968 it was sold for development. But the name Princeville survives.

Although the Princeville shoreline is predominantly sea cliffs, two isolated pocket beaches are located below the Sealodge and Pali Ke Kua condominiums, and one long beach is located at the foot of the Sheraton Princeville Hotel. Six public rights-of-way lead to the Princeville shoreline. Several end at the beaches; the others lead primarily to rocky fishing areas. The rights-of-way are located at Wyllie, Kaweonui, Keoniana, and Kapi'o-lani roads, and at the Pali Ke Kua condominiums and the Sheraton Mirage Princeville Hotel.

Sealodge Beach is most easily reached from the right-of-way in Unit II, a single-family residential area, at the end of Keoniana Road. The trail winds through a thicket of Java plum, guava, and Christmasberry trees and ends at a rocky point. The beach is located a short distance to the west. This is a lovely pocket of coarse white sand. The sand extends inland to the base of the cliffs where a stand of large false *kamani* trees lines the backshore. *Hala* trees cover the steep cliff face above the beach. The nearshore waters are protected by 'Anini Reef, but the wide expanses of the reef end here. To the west of Sealodge Beach the reef is narrow, broken, and irregular. High surf rolls unchecked into the base of the cliffs.

The ocean bottom is shallow and rocky, offering only fair swimming conditions. When the surf is high, powerful rip currents develop. A rip channel is located directly offshore at the reef's edge. During periods of unusually high surf, waves may sweep across the entire beach into the base of the cliffs.

Offshore of Sealodge Beach is a surfing break known as Little Glass Shacks. Its name is a play-on-words of the title of a famous Hawaiian *hapa-haole* song written in 1933, "My Little Grass Shack in Kealakekua, Hawai'i." The "glass shack" is a palatial, many-windowed home on the cliffs above the beach. Little Glass Shacks was a little-known surfing site until October 18, 1985. On that day a Princeville resident, Joe Thomson, was bodyboarding in 4- to 6-foot surf when a large shark attacked his board. Thomson later concluded that poor in-water visibility probably led the shark to mistake his yellow-bottomed bodyboard for a turtle. Sharks feed on turtles and often attack the flippers, one of the turtles' few vulnerable spots. Thomson's hands on the front of the board may have further reinforced his underwater appearance as a turtle floating on the ocean's surface.

Pali Ke Kua Beach is next along the Princeville shoreline. It actually consists of two nearly identical pocket beaches separated by a rocky point. The first of the two is located below the Pali Ke Kua condominiums, and the second is located below the Pu'u Poa condominiums. The nearshore bottom off both beaches is a patchwork of sand pockets and rock, good for both swimming and snorkeling. Large false *kamani* and *hala* trees line the backshores. A picnic pavilion for residents of Pali Ke Kua sits on a terrace above the eastern end of the first beach. The second beach can be reached by walking over the point separating it from the first, or by negotiating a steep and sometimes hazardous dirt trail from the Sheraton Mirage Princeville Hotel parking lot.

The two Pali Ke Kua beaches are protected by patches and fingers of an offshore reef, but occasional high surf generates dangerous water conditions, particularly powerful rip currents, on the reef and in the nearshore waters. During periods of unusually high surf, waves may sweep entirely across the beaches to the base of the cliffs. When the waves are smaller, surfers ride a break offshore called Hideaways.

The third beach at Princeville is Pu'u Poa Beach, lying between the Sheraton Princeville Hotel and the mouth of the Hanalei River. Pu'u Poa, the hill where the hotel is built, was once used as a fish-spotting site. From its heights, a *kilo i'a,* or spotter, would observe the movements of fish schools below him in Hanalei Bay and direct the surround-net operations of the fishermen in their canoes. Sometimes he would signal with a white flag, sometimes with his hands. Similar methods are employed today, but the *kilo i'a* now spots from an airplane and uses two-way radios to communicate with the net fishermen below. The primary catch is still the same—*akule,* or big-eyed scad.

In 1816 the commanding view of Hanalei Bay from Pu'u Poa led to the hill's selection as the site for a Russian fort. Kaumuali'i, the ruling chief of Kaua'i, had traded Hanalei Valley to Dr. Georg Anton Scheffer, a German who was managing Russian trading interests in the islands, for a schooner. Scheffer secretly planned to take over the Hawaiian Islands in the name of Russia and had decided to use Kaua'i as his base of operations. He ordered three forts built, one at Waimea, one at the mouth of Hanalei River, and one on top of Pu'u Poa.

By June of 1817 Scheffer's high-handed conduct had alienated him from the Hawaiians. He was told to leave Kaua'i by Kaumuali'i on orders from King Kamehameha, the ruler of the island chain. Scheffer attempted a final stand at Fort Alexander on Pu'u Poa, but it failed. He and his men sailed to Honolulu and then left the islands.

The ruins of Fort Alexander, named by Scheffer for Tsar Alexander I, are located in the open field between the Sheraton Mirage Princeville Hotel and the hotel's parking lot. Little remains of the structure other than a few mounds of earth and rock foundations. In the years that followed, homes and hotels were built in the same area to take advantage of the spectacular views from the hill. The latest one, the Sheraton Mirage Princeville Hotel, is a 300-room, 60-million-dollar hotel that opened in July 1985.

Pu'u Poa Beach begins at the foot of the hill and ends at the mouth of the Hanalei River. It is a long, moderately wide beach that serves as a natural barrier between Pu'u Poa Marsh and the waters of Hanalei Bay. The backshore of the beach is lined with false *kamani* and ironwood trees and pasture grasses. The marsh is filled with sedge.

An extensive fringing reef protects the nearshore waters. The shallow reef contains many sand pockets and irregular bottom features that offer good snorkeling opportunities. A long, wide, sand-bottomed channel bisects the reef and merges with the beach. The channel flares considerably at the shoreline to form a large swimming area.

Dangerous water conditions occur during periods of high surf, particularly a powerful rip current in the long channel through the reef. High winter waves at the outer edge of the reef provide some of the best surf in the Hawaiian islands. Many surfers compare the Hanalei break with the one at Sunset Beach on the north shore of O'ahu, one of the most famous and challenging surfing sites in the world. The high surf at Hanalei break is for expert surfers only.

Pu'u Poa Beach ends at the mouth of the Hanalei River, where a very shallow sand bar frequently extends completely across the river. Wading across the sand bar from Black Pot Beach Park offers easy access to Pu'u Poa Beach. In winter months, the river occasionally floods after heavy rains, impeding access across the sand bar. No public facilities are available at Pu'u Poa Beach, but they may be found at the beach park.

Black Pot Beach Park

A large group of local people joined the County officiate in celebrating the [dedication of Black Pot Beach

BLACK POT BEACH PARK. A sunbather and her black dog relax on the sand spit at the mouth of the Hanalei River, the site of Black Pot Beach Park. The sand spit often bars the river mouth, preventing the passage of all but shallow-draft boats. The extensive estuary of Hanalei River is famous among Hawaiians for its native biota, including *'o'opu* (goby fish), *'ōpae* (shrimp), and *hīhīwai* (mollusks).

Park] which marked the re-opening of the popular recreation site next to Hanalei Pier.

Formerly a gathering spot for many local people, it derived its name from the big, black cooking pot used by fishermen and picnickers who cooked and shared their fish and stew there.

The "Private Property, No Tresspassing" sign that had been posted for the past seven years was removed at Wednesday's ceremony also, ending the long-standing controversy over the use of the site.

The Garden Island
July 16, 1973

Hanalei means "lei-shaped bay," an appropriate description of this almost perfectly semicircular bay, the largest on Kaua'i. The bay begins at Pu'u Poa in the east and ends at Makahoa Point in the west.

The shoreline of Hanalei Bay is a 2-mile-long crescent of sand which many local residents consider to be the finest beach in the islands. The beach stretches from the mouth of the Hanalei River in the east to Waikoko Reef in the west. A number of small beach parks and rights-of-way are located along its extensive reach.

Black Pot Beach Park is situated at the eastern end of the beach where the Hanalei River meets the ocean.

Adjacent to it is Hanalei Landing, a 300-foot-long pier at the western edge of the park.

At the turn of the century, agriculture was a thriving business in Hanalei Valley. Farmers there were growing and marketing large quantities of rice and needed a commercial landing to facilitate their shipping operations. The pier dates back to the 1890s, but was rebuilt in 1912. A new deck of reinforced concrete replaced the wooden decking in the early 1920s, and at the same time a large warehouse was constructed onshore.

Commercial use of the pier was discontinued in 1933 because California rice growers were by then dominating the market and undercutting the price of Hawaiian rice. Since that time, the pier has been used exclusively for recreational purposes. Diving from the pier is prohibited.

The eastern corner of Hanalei Bay is a traditional gathering place for the residents of Hanalei. Even before the construction of the landing, they congregated here to launch their boats, to fish, to swim, and to socialize. Today, these same activities and others continue at the same site. The name Black Pot predates the development of the public park. For many years a group of Hanalei residents kept a large black cooking pot at the beach, which became a focal point for informal social gatherings and eventually gave the site its popular name.

In December 1967 a group of investors purchased the Black Pot site for $234,000. Although the area had been used continuously by the public for many years, it was private property. The new owners closed the area to the public and announced their intention to build a condominium. Their plans touched off six years of intense controversy. Local residents adamantly refused to give up their traditional recreation site.

By 1973 the developers still had not been able to get the permits needed for their project, and they agreed to sell the parcel to the county for $405,000. In July of that year the area was reopened as Black Pot Beach Park. It is located at the eastern end of Weke Road. Facilities include a comfort station, showers, lifeguard tower, and parking.

The beach park and the pier remain the focal points of ocean recreation in Hanalei and accommodate the following activities: swimming, bodyboarding, surfing, fishing, windsurfing, canoe paddling, and kayaking. A single-lane boat ramp on the west bank of the river is used for both commercial and recreational purposes. Boats are usually able to cross the shallow sand bar at high tide. Immediately offshore of the pier is a midbay anchorage on a sandy bottom at depths of 35 feet. Many yachts and other large boats anchor here during the calm summer months when Hanalei is a popular destination for trans-Pacific and interisland sailors.

During periods of high surf, particularly in the winter and spring months, dangerous water conditions prevail. Powerful rip currents often flow close to the pier, and a pounding shorebreak forms along the entire length of the beach. Over the years, Hanalei Bay has been the site of a number of drownings and near-drownings.

Hanalei Pavilion Beach Park

Hanohano Hanalei i ka ua nui
E pakika kahi limu o Manuʻakepa
I laila hoʻi au i ʻike iho ai
I ka hana huʻi konikoni i ka ʻili
Aloha kahi one o pua rose
I ka hoʻope ʻia e ka hunakai
ʻAkāhi hoʻi au a ʻike i ka nani
Hanohano Hanalei i ka ua nui.

The glory of Hanalei is its heavy rain,
[And its] slippery seaweed of Manuʻakepa
There I felt
A cool, tingling sensation on my skin
Greetings to the sand and the roses
Drenched by the sea spray
Never have I seen such splendor
The glory of Hanalei is its heavy rain.

"Hanohano Hanalei"
Song by Alfred Alohikea
Elbert and Mahoe, 1970

Hanalei Pavilion Beach Park is a popular picnicking site on the shoreline of Hanalei Bay. It is located on Weke Road between Pilikoʻa and Aku roads. As its name indicates, the park's facilities include a picnic pavilion. The original wooden building was destroyed by the tsunami of 1957. The present concrete and hollow tile structure was completed in January 1960.

A popular shorebreak surfing site off the beach park

attracts bodyboarders and surfers. The waves break over a wide, shallow sand bar, offering good opportunities for beginners. High surf, especially common during the winter and spring, generates dangerous water conditions—a pounding shorebreak, a strong backwash, and powerful rip currents. Conditions for swimming are normally better during the calmer summer months, and summer winds attract small catamaran sailors.

Wai'oli Beach Park

Waioli Valley

The scenery in this vicinity is romantically tropical. The soil is fertile, and produces taro, sugar cane, coffee, and indigo, with fruits and vegetables in great variety. This stream, rushing down a rocky chasm, assumes every fantastic shape possible, and a traveler describes it as a picture "more exquisite than any we have seen on the islands."

Hawaiian Guide Book
Whitney, 1875

Wai'oli means "joyful water." It is the name of a land division, a valley, a stream, and a mission house. The Reverend William Alexander established the Wai'oli Mission in Hanalei in 1834 and built the Wai'oli Mission House in 1837. It is located in Hanalei town at its original site, where it was saved from demolition in 1921 and later restored and refurnished.

Offshore of Wai'oli in Hanalei Bay is the site of a famous shipwreck. The ship, *Cleopatra's Barge,* belonged to Liholiho, King Kamehameha II, and was Hawai'i's first royal yacht. Liholiho purchased the elegantly furnished, four-year-old, 83-foot vessel in 1820 for $90,000, and renamed her *Ha'aheo o Hawai'i* ("Pride of Hawai'i"). She went aground on a reef off Wai'oli at the hands of an irresponsible crew.

Wai'oli Beach Park is a small park on the shore of Hanalei Bay. It may be reached from the end of either He'e or 'Ama'ama road. The park's facilities are located in the center of a stand of ironwood trees. Ironwoods have small seed pods that resemble pine cones. For that reason, in Hawai'i, they are commonly, although incorrectly, referred to as pine trees. The botanical accuracy of the name aside, the trees on the beach

are the reason that the shorebreak surfing site at the east end of the park is called Pine Trees. During periods of high surf, other surfing breaks form outside of Pine Trees on Hanalei Bay's inner reefs.

Wai'oli Beach Park and Pine Trees are almost at the midpoint of Hanalei's 2-mile-long beach. High surf, particularly during the winter and spring, seems to focus here and tends to be higher and more powerful than the surf at other sites to the east. The waves break over a wide, shallow sand bar and cause dangerous water conditions, particularly a pounding shorebreak, a strong backwash, and powerful rip currents. Swimming conditions are normally better during the calmer summer months.

The popularity of Pine Trees' waves among expert surfers has made it the major contest site on the north shore of Kaua'i. Bodysurfing, bodyboarding, and surfing contests are all held here annually.

Waikoko Beach

Fifteen persons are dead or missing as the result of a tidal wave which struck Kauai about six-thirty yesterday morning. The north shore of the island took the brunt of the blow, with Wainiha and Haena suffering the heaviest.

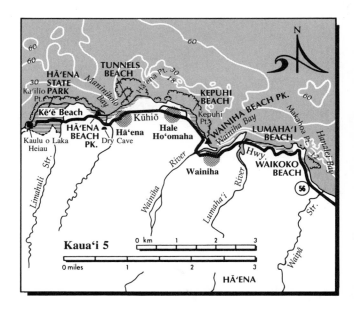

WAIKOKO. Waipā Stream flows into the northwest end of Hanalei Bay, creating pleasant surroundings for sunbathers and picnickers. In the distance at Makahoa Point, Waikoko Reef offers good offshore conditions for surfing and good inshore conditions for snorkeling. This roadside beach borders Kūhiō Highway.

Practically every dwelling in the makai areas of Wainiha, Haena, Kalihikai, Kalihiwai, and Moloaa has either been totally destroyed or damaged to an extent that they are uninhabitable.

With the Waikoko bridge and the Wainiha bridges washed out by the waves, Wainiha and Haena were isolated from the rest of the island.

The Garden Island
April 2, 1946

Waikoko is the name of the westernmost section of Hanalei Bay. It is also the name of a reef which adjoins the beach and of a surfing site at the edge of the reef.

The narrow beach at Waikoko is fronted by Waikoko Reef, a very important shoreline feature. The reef is shallow and wide where it adjoins the shoreline at Makahoa Point. During periods of high surf, it provides excellent protection to the nearshore waters from the dangerous water conditions offshore. For this reason, it is a popular beach for families with children at all times of the year, but particularly during the winter and spring months, the high surf season.

Swimming in the reef shallows is more attractive to children than to adults, but snorkeling opportunities are good for everyone during periods of calm seas. The surfing break, Waikoko, at the outer edge of the reef,

31

offers some excellent waves during the winter surf season. It is primarily a long left slide that attracts expert bodysurfers, bodyboarders, and surfers.

The beach is accessible from the main road, Highway 56. Beachgoers park alongside the road.

Lumaha'i Beach

'Ai wale i ka hinana, ka i'a kaulana o ka 'aina.

Eat readily of the *hinana* [juvenile *'o'opu*], the famous fish of the land.

Traditional saying
Hawaiian Dictionary

Lumaha'i is one of Hawai'i's most scenic beaches. It is three fourths of a mile long, very wide, and backed by lushly vegetated cliffs. Waves surge almost continually across Lumaha'i's sloping foreshore. Its beauty has provided the background for many paintings, advertisements, commercials, and movies, the best known of which was the classic "South Pacific," filmed in 1957.

During the course of the year, Lumaha'i's sands shift dramatically from one end of the beach to the other. During the winter and spring season of high surf, the sand moves from the west to the east; during the summer, the direction is reversed. The width of the beach varies as much as 350 feet with the seasonal changes.

LUMAHA'I. Powerful winter surf rolls into the east end of Lumaha'i Beach, one of Kaua'i's most popular north shore beaches. Unlike other beaches on the island, Lumaha'i has no protective reef so swimmers are often subject to very dangerous water conditions. During periods of high surf the pounding shorebreak, the strong backwash, and the powerful rip currents at this remote site have caused many drownings and near-drownings.

These massive sand movements and the beach's steep foreshore indicate that it is continually assaulted by high surf and strong currents. Unlike many other beaches on Kaua'i, Lumaha'i has no protective reef. It borders the open ocean where the bottom drops immediately to overhead depths. Frequent high surf causes very dangerous water conditions, particularly a pounding shorebreak, a strong backwash, and powerful rip currents. Over the years, the combination of unspoiled shoreline beauty and dangerous ocean, particularly during winter and spring, has proved deadly. Lumaha'i has been the site of innumerable drownings and near-drownings. Drowning victims have included not only swimmers, but also sightseers who have ventured too close to the surf sweeping across the beach or over the rocky margins of the bay. Drowning victims have included people wading in the river at the beach who have been swept out to sea by flash floods. During heavy rains, particularly in the winter and spring, Lumaha'i River is subject to flash floods that within a few minutes cause the river to rise dramatically from a few feet to depths over one's head. In response to the severity of the water safety problem at Lumaha'i Beach, an emergency phone was installed on Kūhiō Highway. Occasionally during the summer, the eastern end of the beach is safe for swimming.

The same surf that has caused so many swimming fatalities attracts expert bodysurfers, bodyboarders, and surfers. The bodysurfers usually ride the shorebreak, whereas the bodyboarders and surfers use a break offshore the western end of the beach where Lumaha'i River meets the ocean. However, when Lumaha'i's surf reaches heights of 6 feet or more, it becomes treacherous and almost no one goes in the water.

Among Hawaiians, Lumaha'i is just as famous for its river as for its beach. The river estuary is an important spawning ground for a native freshwater fish, 'o'opu, a member of the goby family. In a November 11, 1984, newspaper article, *Honolulu Advertiser* staff writer Jan TenBruggencate described 'o'opu in this way:

They come down the streams by the thousands in the freshets of the late summer and fall.

They come to spawn, freshwater fishes preparing to send their offspring through a four-to-seven-month cycle of life in the sea. Then the young will return to the high, cold mountain pools whence came their parents.

The fins on their undersides have fused and turned into kind of a sucker. With these, the 'o'opu young can climb up waterfall faces and stick to rocks in fast moving streams.

Their delicate flesh is so valuable, it can bring nearly $10 a pound.

They are true natives of Hawai'i, an endemic species, having evolved from a saltwater fish into one that spends most of its life in the narrow, rocky streams. And they are found nowhere else in the world.

They are prized by the Hawaiians of old, as they are prized today by Hawai'i's people of many ethnic backgrounds, although the diversion and other modification of streams has made them fairly rare on most of the islands.

You can find them and their close relatives in the fine, babbling brooks of the islands, and particularly on Kaua'i, where many streams still flow unaltered.

Lumaha'i River originates in a narrow valley in the island's central mountains and eventually flows into the ocean at the western end of Lumaha'i Beach. It is the only major river left in Hawai'i that is untouched by development or diversion. The nearly pristine waters of the river and estuary support several varieties of 'o'opu and *hīhīwai* (a native shellfish), and provide a major feeding ground for the *'alae ke'oke'o,* or Hawaiian coot.

Lumaha'i Beach plays a role in maintaining the productivity of the estuary environment. During the summer, when the beach sand shifts to the western end of the beach, it bars the river from flowing into the ocean and stabilizes the estuary. During winter and spring, high surf moves the sand to the opposite end of the beach, often reducing the width of the sand bar at the river mouth by several hundred feet. This erosion, combined with the flooding rains of winter and spring, allows the river to cut easily through the beach and flow into the ocean. And when the river runs into the sea, so do the 'o'opu larvae, by the millions. Within the next few months the surviving larvae mature into *hinana,* juvenile 'o'opu, which find their way back to the Lumaha'i estuary. There they re-acclimate themselves to the fresh water and then swim upstream.

The native 'o'opu that populate Lumaha'i River, were once common in rivers, streams, and estuaries throughout the Hawaiian Islands. *Hinana* would swim by the hundreds of thousands from the ocean back into the streams. When these much-prized young fish were running, people flocked to net them, and despite large catches, they still kept coming. Once caught, they were soaked in salt water for three or four days, dried, and eaten. At other times of the year people fished for adult 'o'opu, one variety of which reportedly reached a foot in length. Today, to prevent over-fishing, weirs are illegal and nets must be sewn with 1.5-inch or bigger eyes.

Lumaha'i Valley, now uninhabited, was once an important agricultural area. It supported a succession of first Hawaiian, then Chinese, and finally Japanese farming communities which grew taro and later rice. The cultivation of rice flourished throughout Kaua'i's north shore from 1890 to 1930. When increased rice production in California eventually led to the demise of the industry in Hawai'i, most rice fields, including those in Lumaha'i Valley, were abandoned. Today, the valley lands are used only as pasture for grazing cattle. The 23-square-mile valley is owned and leased by the Bishop Estate.

Highway 56 separates the beach from the valley. Access to the eastern end of the beach is from several trails originating at the highway. This end of the beach, once called Kahalahala, is the most popular area for sunbathing and swimming during the summer. Access to the western end of the beach is from a roadside parking lot in an ironwood grove along Lumaha'i River.

Wainiha Beach Park

Wainiha Valley is a deep valley which cuts into the heart of Waialeale, a mountain approximately 6,000 feet in height. The valley is about fifteen miles long and receives the under drainage from a large plateau of an elevation of from four to five thousand feet. The Wainiha stream is said to have the most constant flow of any stream on Kauai.

Thrum's Hawaiian Annual
1908

Kaua'i is the only Hawaiian island with an extensive fishery for 'o'opu, native freshwater fishes of the goby family. 'O'opu spend their adult lives in the headwaters of mountain streams, but migrate downstream to spawn. The Wainiha River is one of the focal points of the fishery, providing both the 'o'opu nōpili and the 'o'opu nākea, for fishermen the most prized species. The other three species are 'akupa, naniha, and 'alamo'o. Neighboring Lumaha'i River is another relatively important fishing area. The Hanalei, Waimea, Hanapēpē, and Makaweli rivers produce a large percentage of the island-wide catch, but are not as productive today as in former times.

Fishing is usually best after heavy rains early in the wet season when the adult 'o'opu are migrating downstream, and again some months later when the juveniles are migrating upstream. Highly prized as food by the early Hawaiians, 'o'opu were traditonally caught by extending a small mesh net or a weir across a stream. Today, weirs are illegal to prevent over-fishing and nets must be sewn with 1.5-inch or bigger eyes.

The waters of the Wainiha River, like the waters of most of the rivers on Kaua'i, have been partially diverted for other uses, adversely affecting the 'o'opu population. In Wainiha, the river's waters are compromised by a hydroelectric power plant, which was installed in August 1906 by McBryde Sugar Company to provide electric power to drive irrigation pumps in Hanapēpē. A transmission line carries the electricity 33 miles across the island to Hanapēpē Valley. The plant provides McBryde with half of its electric power and sells its excess to Kaua'i Electric Company.

When operations first began, a wharf was built on the beach and a light railroad was put in up to the powerhouse. Warehouses were also built near the wharf. Today, nothing remains of the coastal structures, for the destructive tsunami of April 1, 1946, that devastated Kaua'i's north shore left little standing on the shoreline at Wainiha.

Wainiha Beach Park borders a long, wide beach at the head of Wainiha Bay. There is no fringing reef in the center of the bay, so the beach is completely exposed to the open ocean. Periods of high surf generate dangerous water conditions, particularly a pounding shorebreak, a strong backwash, and powerful rip currents. Over the years a number of drownings and near-drownings have occurred here.

The waters of the bay are usually murky from the discharge of the Wainiha River at the eastern end of the beach. The combination of hazardous surf conditions and the turbidity of the water discourages most swimmers, but surfers occasionally ride a break along the rocks on the eastern side of the bay. The beach is used primarily by shoreline fishermen and beachcombers.

Kepuhi Beach

Nani wale na hala, 'ea, 'ea
O Naue i ke kai, 'ea, 'ea.

Ke 'oni a'e la, 'ea, 'ea
Pili mai Hā'ena, 'ea, 'ea.

So beautiful are the pandanus
Of Naue by the sea.

Moving there
At Hā'ena.

"Nā Hala o Naue"
Song by J. Kahinu
Elbert and Mahoe, 1970

Kepuhi Beach extends for almost a mile around Kepuhi Point, a long, broad promontory between Wainiha Bay and Hā'ena Point. A series of extensive fringing reefs front the beach, continuing west to Kē'ē Beach at the end of the road. These long sections of wide, flat, shallow reefs provide some of the best fishing on the north shore.

One of the most popular methods of fishing practiced here is throw-netting. Contrary to popular belief, throw-net fishing, although whole-heartedly adopted by the Hawaiians, was not native to them, but was introduced by the Japanese. In March 1974, *Honolulu Advertiser* staff writer Mary Cooke interviewed Harry Okamura, a Japanese throw-net fisherman who was born in 1900 at Koloa, Kaua'i, and was raised at Anahola. Okamura told the interviewer, " I learned throw-net fishing from old-time Japanese when I was eight years old. I used to see Japanese teaching Hawaiians how to make the nets and throw them. The Hawaiians had lay or gill nets that were made of native fiber." Okamura concluded the interview by saying that Kaua'i has "nice, wide, long reefs for throw-netting. That's still about the best island for this kind of fishing."

When a throw net is cast over a school of fish, it flares open into a full circle just before it drops into the water. *'Upena ho'olei,* one of the Hawaiian names for a throw-net, is a poetic description of the flight and movement of the net. *'Upena* means "net," and *ho'olei* means both "to put a lei on someone" and "to throw." The technique of throwing the net is only one factor that determines a fisherman's success. Probably more important for productive throw-netting is the fisherman's understanding of the habits and the movements of fish that he is after.

A flat, shallow reef is known as a *papa* or more commonly on Kaua'i as an *'āpapa.* Many of the popular fish that inhabit these reefs, such as *moi, āholehole, manini, kala,* and *nenue,* have distinct and predictable feeding habits. They usually move into the deeper waters with the outgoing tide and return with the incoming tide, and they usually swim over the same *ala,* the roads or channels through the reef. When they are at a certain reef, they usually move between three or four *hale,* or houses, as they feed. A successful throw-net fisherman, like a successful hunter, must take all these factors into account as well as others, including the surf, the season, the weather, and his days off from work. When everything has come together to his satisfaction, he can be seen with his net over his shoulder, crouched patiently at one of his favorite sites on the reef, waiting for the school of fish he has spotted to approach.

In recent years, much to the dismay of the throw-net fishermen, many of their favorite reefs have become popular snorkeling, surfing, and windsurfing sites. The schools of fish for which they patiently wait are often scattered by a windsurfer zipping by or by a surfer paddling out to the break at the edge of the reef. The Hawaiians use the term *hōkai* to describe these disturbances that scare the fish away. The fishermen themselves are objects of curiosity, and visitors strolling on the beach often approach them to see what they are doing or to take a picture. Although many of the easily accessible reefs have been compromised by other ocean recreation enthusiasts, fortunately for the fishermen on Kaua'i, there are still a number of remote sites left where throw-net fishing can be practiced undisturbed.

Widespread recreational and subsistence activities on Hawaiian reefs have been the origin of many individual place names both offshore and onshore. Some of the names still remembered along Kepuhi Beach are: Wainiha Kuau, the first reef at the edge of Wainiha Bay; Kepuhi, the beach and the point; Kaʻōnohi, the point where Camp Naue is located; Naue, the backshore at the point, famous in songs and chants for its *hala,* or pandanus, grove; Wāwaekāhaʻi and Kapaiki, the reefs east and west of Camp Naue; and Kanahā, the next big reef that adjoins Hāʻena Point.

Kepuhi Beach is fronted by alternating sections of shallow reef and deep channels. High surf often causes dangerous water conditions, particularly strong waves surging across the shallow reefs and powerful rip currents running out through the channels. Over the years, a number of drownings and many near-drownings have occurred here. Public rights-of-way are located along Highway 56 and on Alamoʻo and Ālealea roads.

Tunnels Beach

Henry Gomez was born in 1913 not far from the then new power plant in Wainiha Valley. He has fished the north shore of Kauai since he was only three or four years old. He knows every reef and fishing spot from Na Pali east past Moloaa.

"Back in the old days, if I would say to another fisherman, I had caught nenue at Makua, he'd know just where to go to fish. Today, it is known as 'Tunnels,' " said Gomez.

Kauai Times
1988

Tunnels Beach, one of the north shore's most popular ocean recreation sites, is located at Hāʻena Point. Much of the shoreline at the point is lined by beachrock or naturally cemented sand, an unappealing feature for swimmers. Offshore of the beach, however, is a massive hook-shaped reef that accommodates many other activities. The reef, formerly known as Mākua, contains a deep lagoon within its hook that serves as a summer anchorage, primarily for sailing craft, and as a fishing and snorkeling site during periods of calm seas. Large boats enter from Mākua Channel, a wide channel to the west. Smaller, shallow-draft boats, especially inflatables, can also enter from the east through Kanahā Channel, a narrow channel that separates Kanahā Reef at the eastern edge of Hāʻena Point from Mākua Reef.

During the winter and spring, high surf generates dangerous water conditions, particularly powerful rip currents that flow west through the lagoon and out through Mākua Channel into Hāʻena Bay. High surf also creates a surfing break called Tunnels at the outer corner of the reef. This break, for experts only, attracts both surfers and windsurfers. Windsurfers come out through Kanahā Channel any time the wind is strong, whether or not surf is breaking. Although high winter surf precludes most in-water activities, it also makes for good beachcombing because waves washing across Hāʻena Point deposit a great deal of debris onshore, including a wide variety of shells.

During periods of calm seas, net and spear fishermen dive in many areas of the reef, particularly the lagoon. The divers named the site Tunnels for the many arches and tunnels that are found along the inner slope of the reef surrounding the lagoon. Surfers have always assumed that the name came from the tubular or tunnel-shaped waves at the surfing break, but the name predated the use of the reef as a surfing site.

Tunnels Beach is accessible from two public rights-of-way to Hāʻena Point—one on the east side of the point and one on the west. The east right-of-way is especially well used by windsurfers, who have a considerable amount of equipment to carry to the water; so a beach access that puts them close to their sailing site is always popular. They consider Tunnels Beach one of the best sailing sites on Kauaʻi. The west right-of-way is popularly used by sunbathers, snorkelers, and surfers.

Hāʻena Beach Park

ʻAlu aku i ke kula a ʻo Hāʻena
Nā hala o Naue, nā hala o Naue
Wehiwehi o Luluʻupali.

Accompany us to the plain of Hāʻena
(To see) the (famous) pandanus grove of Naue
(The) adornment of (the cliff) Luluʻupali.

"Nā Uʻi o Kauaʻi"
Traditional song

Hawaiian fishermen know the beach and the bay at Hāʻena Beach Park as Maniniholo, the "traveling *manini* fish." In former times, this area was a popular *hukilau* site, particularly during the months of July and

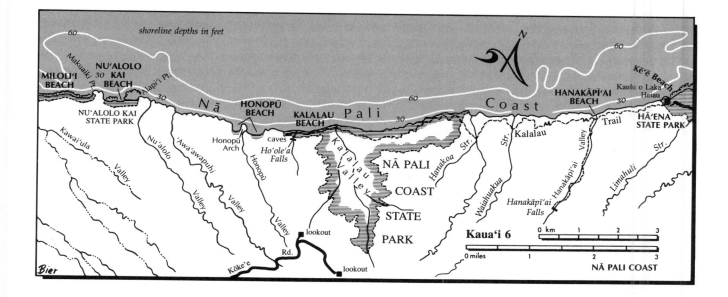

August when the ocean is usually calm. Today the *huki-lau*-style of net fishing is rarely seen. Maniniholo is also the name of the dry cave across the highway from the park. The cave, a lava tube that runs several hundred feet inland, was once a sea cave when the level of the ocean was substantially higher than it is now. Waves that pounded into the cave enlarged the entrance to its present size.

Hā'ena Beach Park occupies the low, vegetated sand dunes located along the backshore of Maniniholo Beach. The wide bay offshore is bordered by two large reefs, Mākua Reef to the east and Hauwā Reef to the west, but no reef protects the beach itself. It is completely exposed to the open ocean. During periods of high surf, particularly during the winter and spring, waves funnel unchecked directly into the beach, creating very dangerous water conditions, particularly a pounding shorebreak, a strong backwash, and powerful rip currents. The foreshore of the beach is always steep, a good indication of the erosive force of the annual high surf. Over the years Hā'ena Beach Park has been the site of a number of drownings and many near-drownings. Swimmers and bodysurfers in the shorebreak are usually the victims.

The park and its public facilities are located on Highway 56 across the road from Maniniholo Dry Cave.

Hā'ena State Park

Ha'ena, o keia ka wahi i noho ai o Lohiau ma ka huli mauka o ka Pali o Makana.

Ha'ena was the place where Lohiau lived on the inland face of Pali o Makana.

"Kaua'i Place Names"
Kelsey Collection

Hā'ena, "red hot," is the westernmost land division in the district of Hanalei, one of the five major districts on Kaua'i. Hā'ena's coastal region consists of a narrow strip of flatlands that begin at Wainiha Bay and end at Kē'ē Beach. Highway 56, the only road in and out of the area, also ends here at Kē'ē. The end of the road marks the beginning of the famous Nā Pali Coast State Park, a vast coastal wilderness, accessible only by boat or trail, that includes a series of beautiful coastal valleys.

Hā'ena State Park consists of 230 acres of beachfront lands situated between Limahuli Stream to the east and Nā Pali Coast State Park to the west. Mostly undeveloped, Hā'ena State Park includes a large number of ancient ruins of archaeological importance. Hawaiians fished and farmed here as early as A.D. 1000, and many remnants of their habitation sites, such as house platforms, agricultural terraces, and *heiau,* can still be seen.

37

HāʻENA STATE PARK. Kēʻē Beach, one of the most popular snorkeling sites on Kauaʻi's north shore, is located at the west end of Hāʻena State Park. Visitors drive from all parts of the island to snorkel in the small, protected lagoon offshore the beach. Many species of common reef fish are abundant including wrasses *(hīnālea),* butterflyfish, damselfish, goatfish *(weke),* convictfish *(manini),* and surgeonfish *(kole).*

Despite the park's rich pre-contact archaeological resources, it is probably best known for a modern settlement within its boundaries that was called Taylor Camp, named for the owner of the land at the time, Howard Taylor, brother of actress Elizabeth Taylor.

Taylor Camp was associated with the hippie movement of the late 1960s and the early 1970s. These young American mostly suburbanites who had rejected con-temporary economic and social values as superficial were experimenting with alternative lifestyles, particularly a return to the simplicity of subsistence living.

Many of these hippies had heard that Hawaiʻi was a tropical paradise that offered ideal opportunities to live off the land. During the late 1960s, they began arriving in Hawaiʻi in droves. When a large encampment of them was evicted from Hanamāʻulu Beach Park, north shore landowner Howard Taylor offered them a camp-site on his property. The fame of this Taylor Camp spread, attracting a steady flow of "flower children." At its maximum size, the camp was home to more than 80 permanent and 50 transient residents living in tents, tree houses, and semipermanent shacks in a wooded area on the west bank of Limahuli Stream. Amenities included a communal shower, an open-air toilet, a small church, and a cooperative store.

As with many other hippie communities, however, the return to the land at Taylor Camp was itself superficial and only marginally successful at best. Most of the residents depended on regular trips to the store to subsist, and many financed these trips with money obtained from sales of drugs and from welfare funds. In 1972 the state began condemnation proceedings to acquire the land as part of Hāʻena State Park. Taylor and the camp residents protested. Nevertheless, the court ruled in favor of the state, but with the proviso that the evicted campers be given relocation assistance. The state finally took over in 1977.

Taylor Camp is probably best remembered as the original home of the *puka* shell. The Hāʻena shoreline is one of the best shelling areas on Kauaʻi, and cone shells are common. The north shore's heavy winter surf often breaks the tops off the little cones and erodes a hole through them. The hippies at Taylor Camp discovered them and named them *puka* shells. *Puka* is the Hawaiian word for hole. A young woman living in the camp fashioned an anklet of the shells by simply stringing them together. Soon almost everyone was making simple jewelry of all kinds.

According to the popular story of the beginning of the international *puka* shell craze, Howard Taylor gave a necklace of the shells to his famous sister Liz. She wore it in public and created an overnight demand in fashionable circles for *puka* shell jewelry. Soon the jewelry was commanding very high prices in trend-setting fashion shops across the nation. Hawaii went crazy trying to meet the demand. Nearly every white sand beach in the state was scoured and sifted many times over for the now precious shells. In 1974 they were selling for $6.00 per pound, and by this time the shell hunters included local residents as well as hippies. The craze finally subsided when mass-produced plastic imitations

began appearing on the market. Prices for the real thing plummeted, and so did interest. Another American craze had come and gone.

The beach that borders the state park begins at Hāʻena Beach Park on the east, fronts a number of privately owned shoreline properties, and ends at Kēʻē. Like many other north shore coastal areas, this beach is protected by a number of well-developed fringing reefs, all of which were important to Hawaiians for fishing and gathering. The Hawaiians gave place names to all of their food gathering sites, some of which are still remembered. Hauwā is the large, very shallow reef that begins at the western edge of Hāʻena Bay; surfers call it Cannons. The waves that break here are so hollow that they often "spit" out a blast of compressed air and sea spray, and early surfers who rode the break likened the blast to the firing of a cannon. Inshore of Hauwā is a rock formation on the sand that was known as Halepō-haku.

The next reef is Puʻu Kahuaiki; the surfing spot there is called Bobo's. Many north shore residents believe that it was named for Bobo Hawk, a former Taylor Camp resident, who was a good bodysurfer and a strong ocean swimmer. However, the name predates her arrival in the early 1970s. The original Bobo was apparently a local surfer who discovered the break in the 1960s. To the west is another reef, Puʻu Kahuanui, portions of which are emergent even at high tide.

The channel cut through the reef by Limahuli Stream was called Poholokeiki. This was also the name of the shoreline area where Taylor Camp was located. The large fringing reef offshore was known as Kaʻilio, the eastern end being Kaʻilioiki and the section at the point, Kaʻilionui. Although its meaning is now uncertain, *kaʻilio* may be an abbreviated form of *kai ʻilio* which may mean either a type of seaweed or a seal. In former times, seals were known regularly to beach themselves here. Kaʻilio is the name commonly used for the entire point and its adjoining beach. Windsurfers know the area as Reefers.

Kēʻē marks the western end of many things: the reef, the beach, the road, and the park. The large reef that begins at Kaʻilio Point ends here in a small, sand-bottomed lagoon. The lagoon, separated from the open ocean by a shallow, but wide, reef flat, offers a protected, nearshore swimming site. The lagoon makes Kē'ē Beach the most popular swimming and snorkeling site in Hā'ena State Park. During periods of high surf, particularly during the winter and spring, dangerous water conditions occur nearshore. At such times, a powerful rip current runs out to sea through a channel penetrating the western end of the reef flat. Over the years, this channel has been the site of a number of drownings and many near-drownings. During periods of calm seas, spear fishermen, kayakers, and snorkelers occasionally use the channel to reach the open ocean beyond the reef. Recreational swimmers, however, would be well advised to avoid the channel at all times of the year. A current flows through it no matter what the surf conditions are.

The same dangerous high surf conditions that occur at Kē'ē are found in the other channels through the reefs at Ka'ilio Point. The surfing and windsurfing sites offshore of the point are for experts only. Recreational swimmers and snorkelers should exercise a great deal of caution in these areas, even during the calmer summer months when strong currents can be generated by trade winds and tidal changes.

The house on the point adjoining Kē'ē Beach was last privately owned by John Allerton. Upon his death in 1986, it was acquired by the state. On the hill west of the Allerton house are several important archaeological sites associated with the hula. These include Ke Ahu o Laka, a platform where the hula was performed; Kauluapaoa Heiau, a temple dedicated to Laka, the goddess of the hula; and a house site. These sites are also associated with legends of Hi'iaka, the sister of Pele, the volcano goddess, and Lohi'au, Pele's lover.

Nā Pali Coast State Park

The sun was just rising when we reached the point where the great palis or precipices begin. These precipices are one of the grandest wonders of the Islands, but the danger of examining them on the passage deters many persons from visiting them. There are those who will travel by land sixty miles around rather than sail these fifteen by canoe, and I was warned not to try. But with me curiosity was stronger than caution.

"Journal of a Canoe Voyage along the Kauai Palis, Made in 1845"
Gilman, 1908

Nā Pali Coast State Park encompasses 6,500 acres of exceptionally beautiful sea cliffs and coastal valleys. Nā Pali, meaning "the cliffs," describes the 15 miles of isolated shoreline between Kē'ē Beach and Polihale Beach. Nā Pali's coastal wildernesses provide excellent opportunities for day-hiking, backpacking, camping, amateur archaeological explorations, and nature walks. The coastal waters and reefs support a variety of ocean recreation activities, including swimming, bodysurfing, surfing, snorkeling, spear fishing, and boating. Periods of high surf, particularly during the winter and spring, generate very dangerous water conditions throughout the park, the cause of many drownings and near drownings.

There are five major sand beaches within Nā Pali Coast State Park. They are located at Hanakāpī'ai, Kalalau, Honopū, Nu'alolo Kai, and Miloli'i. The first two are accessible from the Kalalau Trail.

The Kalalau Trail, a Hawaiian coastal trail, begins at Kē'ē Beach and traverses Nā Pali's steep sea cliffs and coastal valleys for 11 miles before terminating at Kalalau Beach. Veteran hikers pushing hard can cover the distance in five hours, but most people elect to follow a more leisurely pace, often taking an entire day or more to reach the end. The trail's first stop is at Hanakāpī'ai Beach, 2 miles in from the trail head. From Hanakāpī'ai, the trail climbs abruptly and does return to sea level until it reaches Kalalau Beach.

The remaining beaches—Honopū, Nu'alolo Kai, and Miloli'i—are accessible only from the ocean. During summer periods of calm seas, strong swimmers occasionally swim from Kalalau Beach to Honopū's twin beaches, but Nu'alolo Kai and Miloli'i can be reached only by boat. Swimmers should watch for man-o-war, the stinging jellyfish that are blown ashore by strong trade winds.

Nā Pali Coast State Park is managed by the Division of State Parks. Camping is allowed by permit at Hanakāpī'ai, Hanakoa (along the trail), Kalalau, and Miloli'i. Permits may be obtained at the state park's office in Līhu'e. Permits are not required for day hikes to Hanakāpī'ai.

Whether you are planning a walk to Hanakāpī'ai or a hiking expedition to Kalalau, remember the following points:

Nā Pali Coast State Park. Miloli'i Beach, the westernmost of the five wilderness beaches in Nā Pali Coast State Park, is a beachcomber's delight. High surf, particularly during the winter and spring, deposits large amounts of debris onshore including a wide variety of shells. The narrow fringing reef fronting the beach provides good opportunities for spear fishing and, on occasion, for surfing.

• You are in a wilderness park. There are no life-guards or rangers. Professional rescue assistance can be obtained only if someone hikes out to get help or signals a passing boat or helicopter. Even if rescue personnel are dispatched, by the time they actually arrive at the scene of the incident it will likely be too late for the victim—particularly for ocean incidents. You are responsible for your actions. If you act irresponsibly, you may find yourself in a life-threatening situation.

• During periods of heavy rains, particularly during the winter and spring, streams rise and flash floods occur without warning. Do not cross a flooded stream. Wait for the water to subside.

• Goat hunting with firearms is permitted along the Kalalau Trail during August and September from Hanakoa to Kalalau. Confine your hiking to the main trail when hunters are in the area.

Hanakāpī'ai Beach

Ka 'o'opu peke o Hanakāpī'ai.
The short *'o'opu* of Hanakāpī'ai.

The *'o'opu* at Hanakāpī'ai on Kaua'i were said to be shorter and plumper than those anywhere else. Famed in legends and mentioned in chants. Sometimes applied humorously to a short, plump person.

'Ōlelo No'eau, Hawaiian Proverbs and Poetical Sayings
Pukui, 1983

Hanakāpī'ai is one of Kaua'i's most popular wilderness day-hike destinations. It is located 2 miles from Kē'ē Beach, a 1.5-hour walk for most hikers. The valley once supported a Hawaiian fishing and farming community. Habitation sites are found in the valley and agricultural terraces extend nearly a mile inland from the beach.

During the late 1800s, W. E. H. Deverill, a resident of Hanalei, planted thousands of coffee trees in the valley. A 2-mile-long trail to Hanakāpī'ai Falls at the head of the valley leads past many of the trees and the ruins of Deverill's coffee mill.

Hanakāpī'ai Beach is a pocket beach at the mouth of the valley. During periods of calm seas, especially during the summer, sand covers the boulders at the shoreline. Recreational swimmers and snorkelers should exercise caution even when the ocean appears safe because there is no reef offshore to protect the beach, and longshore currents generated by the trade winds and tidal changes commonly flow past the valley.

During the winter and spring, a dramatic change occurs at Hanakāpī'ai. High surf assaults the entire Nā Pali coast and completely erodes the pocket of sand. The waves carry the sand offshore, exposing a boulder beach subject to a pounding shorebreak, backwash, undertows, turbid waters, cross-waves off the cliffs, very powerful rip currents, and strong longshore currents.

All of these dangerous water conditions have proved to be extremely hazardous to day-hikers who visit the beach. Many drownings and near-drownings have occurred here. During the period from 1970 to 1979, there were twelve drownings, five of them in 1979 alone. The victims are invariably out-of-state visitors unaware of the dangers of Hawaii's surf and currents. Occasionally, local bodysurfers ride the waves at Hanakāpī'ai. If you are not an expert in Hawaiian surf, however, do not attempt to join them. Remember, you are in a wilderness park. There are no lifeguards or rangers. Professional rescue assistance can be summoned only by someone who hikes out or signals a passing boat or helicopter. Even if rescue personnel are dispatched, by the time they actually reach Hanakāpī'ai, it will probably be too late for the victim, particularly for ocean incidents. You are responsible for your actions. If you act irresponsibly, you may find yourself or your family in a life-threatening situation.

Kalalau Beach

Aia ka makani la i Kauai,
He Lawakua ko Napali,
He Lanikuuwaa ko Kalalau,
He Lauae ko Honopu,
He Aikoo ko Nualolo,
He Makani Kuehu Kai ko Milolii.

The winds of Kauai are:
The Lawakua of Napali,
The Lanikuuwaa of Kalalau,
The Lauae of Honopu,
The Aikoo of Nualolo,
The Kuehu Kai of Milolii.

Hawaiian Antiquities and Folklore
Fornander, 1918

Kalalau is the most famous wilderness shoreline hiking destination in Hawai'i. The valley and its adjoining beach lie at the end of the Kalalau Trail, an arduous 11-mile trail that begins at Kē'ē Beach and ends at Kalalau Beach. Every year hundreds of hikers walk for six to ten hours, or more, over the winding trail that leads to this remote site, then spend several days enjoying a wilderness camping experience before they hike out. Many other adventurers elect to make the journey to and from this Nā Pali valley on one of the commercial boats that shuttle passengers and tours along the coast from May to September.

Most of the hiking and camping activity takes place during the summer months when the trail and the camping sites are usually dry and when the ocean is comparatively calm. During the winter and spring, heavy rains make the trail muddy and slippery, and high surf makes all in-water activities, including boating, extremely dangerous.

The beach and valley at Kalalau are part of Nā Pali Coast State Park, 6,500 acres of sea cliffs and valleys between Kē'ē and Mākaha Valley. Most of this coast was designated as a forest reserve in 1907, but Kalalau was excluded because it was in agricultural use by Hawaiians who were still living in the valley and growing taro. Their small community even had a school and a church that the missionaries established in the 1800s. With the coming of Western civilization, however, native people throughout the islands began moving toward the port cities where life was more exciting. The smaller, more isolated valleys were the first to be deserted, and the larger ones, such as Kalalau, were also eventually abandoned.

In 1949 an archaeological survey team spent two weeks in Kalalau. They were accompanied by John Hanohano who had been born in Kalalau, had lived there until he was eleven, and had been taking visitors to and from the valley on his sampan for most of his adult life. From a fascinating series of interviews with Hanohano, Tiare Emory, one of the team members, recorded Hanohano's memories of Hawaiian life in Kalalau.

Hanohano said that the last inhabitants of Kalalau left in 1919. The turn of the century had been a time of transition for them. They lived in *pili*-grass houses until the end, but they were all already wearing European clothes made of cloth. They still used blankets made of tapa from the *wauke,* or paper mulberry, tree that was abundant in the plateau above Ho'ole'a Falls at the western end of the beach. Some of their traditional implements, such as poi pounders, grinders, and fishing sinkers were still made of stone, but almost everything else was of foreign manufacture and made of metal, including needles, axes, knives, and fishhooks. They used wooden canoes with sails to trade their taro with the people of Ni'ihau, Hanalei, and Waimea, but money was the medium of exchange.

The most exciting time of the year was the fishing season from April to July, when tides were low, the ocean was usually calm, and the caves at the western end of the beach were filled with sand. All of the valley residents would come down and camp at the caves. A spotter would be positioned on the bluffs above Ho'ole'a Falls. When he saw a school of fish nearing the beach, he would call to the fishermen below. They would launch a canoe, surround the school with a net, and then pull the net in to shore in the *hukilau* style of fishing.

Western civilization finally caught up with Kalalau. The young people left to look for jobs and were gone for long periods of time. Life was hard and lonely for the older people left behind. Eventually, the older family members followed their children, and by 1919 the valley was deserted.

In 1920, valley lands in Kalalau and elsewhere along Nā Pali were leased to ranchers for pasturage. Within 10 years, the cattle had caused such severe erosion by trampling and denuding the vegetation that all of the leases were canceled. At Kalalau, however, the Robinson family of Ni'ihau owned 150 acres of land and continued ranching there. It was difficult because the cattle, the horses, and the cowboys all had to be barged in and out from the Robinson's ranch in Makaweli, but they continued operations in the valley until the 1970s. At that time, the state acquired full control of Kalalau and turned its management over to the Division of State Parks.

During the late 1960s and the early 1970s, while the land acquisition issues in Kalalau were being resolved, the valley became a refuge for hippies. Many of these young people were invading the islands in search of a place to live off the land and they soon found their way to Kalalau. Their increasing numbers spoiled the valley for the famous "Hermit of Kalalau," Dr. Bernard Wheatley. He left in 1969, after spending six years alone in the valley. By the end of the 1970s, dozens of people were living permanently in the valley, and during the summer months the population soared to well over 100. Public access by trail and landings by helicopters and boats were at that time unrestricted. Accumulation of trash and lack of sanitation facilities became serious problems.

In 1980 the Division of State Parks brought the situation under control through a management plan requiring all campers to obtain a permit and limiting the number of permits issued for any given day. Helicopter landings are now prohibited and boat landings are regulated. Sanitation facilities and a central trash disposal pit are located near the shoreline camping sites. These controls and improvements have helped to re-establish and enhance the value of the valley as a wilderness destination.

The focal point of the valley is Kalalau Beach, a long, wide beach backed by low, vegetated sand dunes. Camping in Kalalau is permitted only at the shoreline; so most of the social activity naturally centers here. Drinking water comes from Ho'ole'a Falls at the western end of the beach. The Division of State Parks recommends that all water be boiled or treated before it is used for drinking or cooking. During the summer, sand fills the large sea caves west of the falls, providing additional camping sites. Campers seeking shelter in the caves should be alert to the possibility of landslides. In July 1980, a rock ledge above the caves broke loose after a heavy rainfall and set off a massive landslide into the shoreline below. The campers in the caves luckily escaped serious injuries. The caves are also home to a number of Hawaiian noddies, or *noio*. These small black terns with gray foreheads get their English name from the way they nod their heads on land.

During periods of calm seas, especially during the summer, the beach attracts many swimmers, but caution is urged even when the ocean appears safe. A wide, moderately shallow sand bar parallels almost the entire length of the beach, but the ocean bottom drops abruptly in many places to overhead depths. There is no reef offshore to protect the beach, and longshore currents generated by the trade winds and tidal changes commonly flow past the valley.

During the winter and spring, high surf assaults the entire Nā Pali coast, eroding the shoreline, reducing the volume of sand onshore, and carrying away all of the sand from the sea caves at the western end of the beach. The surf creates a pounding shorebreak on the sand bar, backwash, undertows, turbid waters, cross-waves off the cliffs, rip currents, and strong longshore currents. A particularly fast and dangerous rip current runs out to sea from the center of the beach. Its plume of agitated water and sand is easily visible from the bluffs above.

Over the years, all of these dangerous water conditions have been the cause of many drownings and near-drownings here. The victims are invariably out-of-state visitors who are unaware or have no regard for the dangers of Hawaii's surf and currents. Occasionally, local bodysurfers and surfers ride the waves at Kalalau, but if you are not an expert in Hawaiian surf, do not attempt to join them. Remember, you are in a wilderness park. There are no lifeguards or rangers. Professional rescue assistance can be summoned only by someone hiking out or signaling a passing boat or helicopter. Even if rescue personnel are dispatched, by the time they actually reach Kalalau, it will probably be too late for the victim, particularly in an ocean incident. You are responsible for your actions. If you act irresponsibly, you may find yourself or your family in a life-threatening situation.

Honopū Beach

At 8:25 we arrived off Honopu and here discovered that, although the sea was smooth, a fair sized ground swell was running. The first boat to attempt landing from the sampan got into an argument with a breaker, and before the argument was finished the boat was half full of water. This experience led to more caution, and the rest of the landing was safely accomplished.

Honolulu Advertiser
July 20, 1922

Honopū, "conch bay," is the most picturesque and the most photographed of all the Nā Pali beaches. Tucked into the base of a high sea cliff, Honopū Beach is actually a pair of wide pocket beaches separated by a thick wall of lava. A huge arch cut by wave action through the wall allows direct access from one beach to the other. Sand dunes fill the backshores of both beaches.

Former *Honolulu Advertiser* editor Lorrin Thurston offered this discription of the area in 1922 in an article entitled "The Kingdom of Nualolo":

No finer beach camp site can be found in the islands than under the huge Honopu Arch, which divides two as perfect bathing beaches as exist in Hawaii. The arch itself is almost 65 feet high and 200 feet wide. The distance from one beach to the other is 182 feet.

A waterfall drops from the Honopu Valley floor about a hundred feet to the beach, the water running thence through the arch and empties into the sea on the far side.

There is a great abundance of drift wood lodged in the rocks back from the beach, relics of past storms. The arch is wide enough to protect campers at all times from the rain, and a cool wind sweeps through it, which makes a blanket comfortable every night.

Honopū's beautiful beaches are a scant half-mile to the west of Kalalau Beach, but there is no overland access from Kalalau to Honopū. During periods of calm seas, primarily during the summer, strong swimmers reach Honopū by swimming along the sea cliffs. However, if you do not have fins and you are not an experienced open-ocean swimmer, do not attempt the swim. The prevailing trade wind current runs west, away from Kalalau. Remember, Nā Pali Coast State Park is a wilderness park. There are no lifeguards or rangers. Professional rescue assistance can be summoned only by someone hiking out or signaling a passing boat or helicopter. Make your decisions very carefully. Camping is not permitted at Honopū.

During the winter and spring, high surf assaults the

entire Nā Pali coast, eroding Honopū's beaches, reducing the volume of sand onshore, and often completely inundating the twin beaches. The surf also creates a pounding shorebreak, backwash, undertows, turbid waters, cross-waves off the cliffs, rip currents, and strong longshore currents. The swim to Honopū from Kalalau should never be attempted during periods of high surf.

Honopū Valley, a hanging valley, the valley floor of which is 150 feet above its twin beaches, is popularly known as the Valley of the Lost Tribe. The best account of the Lost Tribe legend was given by Jan TenBruggencate, the *Honolulu Advertiser's* Kaua'i Bureau columnist. In a 1985 article entitled "A Lost Tribe, a Lonely Valley—A Legend from Kauai," he commented, "It's all a mistake, but it's a catchy legend, and after all these years, it's unlikely the facts will get in its way."

Apparently, the references to the Lost Tribe began in 1922 after an exploratory expedition from the Bishop Museum had visited the remote valley. One of the archaeologists found several skulls that he believed were not Hawaiian, but were those of a primitive, pre-Hawaiian people. His find and theory were publicized, and the legend of the Lost Tribe was off and running. Subsequent archaeological studies of the valley and its artifacts have determined that all of its residents were clearly Hawaiian, but the legend, in several versions, still endures.

Nu'alolo Kai Beach

When we had passed about two-thirds of the pali we came to a little bay making in between two arms or points of land, on the shore of which we noticed several canoes, and a few miserable huts. . . . The little bay is a gathering place for canoes passing between Waimea and Hanalei, as well as those that go over to the island of Niihau, which can be seen here at a distance of about 25 miles.

A few rods back from the beach rise the cliffs, in some places perpendicular for 500 feet, forming an amphitheater. Along the base of one side are ranged the houses, which form a striking contrast with the black mass of rock rising behind them. All their food comes from above, where it is said there is a fine valley (Nualolo) which the feet of white men have never profaned.

"Journal of a Canoe Voyage along the Kauai Palis, Made in 1845"
Gilman, 1908

Nu'alolo Kai is a part of the Nā Pali Coast State Park. Here, the shoreline portion of the park occupies a narrow coastal flat that is bounded by steep sea cliffs. On the coastal flat, which covers an area 3,000 feet long and 250 feet wide, was once a small Hawaiian fishing village. By the turn of the twentieth century, this community was gone. Its residents had left their remote valley home and moved to more populous parts of the island. Today, only the ruins of their habitation sites and a *heiau*, or temple, remain.

The eastern point of the bay at Nu'alolo is a high, vertical sea cliff. It was up the face of this cliff that a trail once led from Nu'alolo Kai ("Nu'alolo [of the] sea"), the fishing village at sea level, to Nu'alolo 'Āina ("Nu'alolo [of the] land"), the heavily terraced valley on the plateau above. The trail was described by G. E. Gilman in 1845:

As we came along, I had noticed a ladder placed against the face of the cliff, for the purpose of reaching the heights above. A native presented himself as a guide, and I let him lead the way. Starting off, I had no doubt that I was going to ascend the ladder at once, but I had taken but a few steps before I found myself halting and reconnoitering. The way which had appeared so easy, now showed itself full of danger.

The path had been excavated by the natives with their rude tools, from the face of an overhanging cliff. It is not level, but is formed like a gouge turned edgewise, so that one's hold is very precarious. It is also too low to admit of any other than a stooping posture, and I was obliged to shuffle along with the utmost caution. My guide seemed quite at home, as he stood upright outside of me, with his body projecting beyond the surface of the cliff, and encouraged me on.

I had taken off my shoes, and by degrees had worked myself two-thirds past, when I rested for a survey. There I was, my chief support a little projecting stone, not sufficient to afford a hold for my whole foot, and my hands clinging with a death grip to the rock, and in this situation overhanging a gulf that was foaming and boiling, as the surf broke over the rocks sixty or seventy feet below me, and which would have proved my death place, if I had made the least mistake or slip. I had strong curiosity to go forward, but discretion prevailed, and I returned. I was then told that few white men had gone as far as I had, and that none had ever passed up the ladder. . . . I can only wonder that there is not an accident every day.

45

The inevitability of an accident on the perilous cliff trail to Nuʻalolo ʻĀina apparently inspired a Hawaiian legend, the legend of the Rainbow Princess. The story was told this way in Armitage and Judd's *Ghost Dog and Other Hawaiian Legends:*

A family of Hawaiians were moving into the valley of Nualolo on the Napali coast. To reach this valley it was necessary to climb on a swinging ladder which hung over the cliff. One man was carrying a baby girl, and as he swung on to the swaying ladder he dropped the child. The parents, in agony, watched their baby falling but were overjoyed to see the *akua* of the rainbow catch her up before she struck the water and carry her on the rainbow over the mountains down to Waimea Valley.

In Waimea, the story goes on, under the protection and care of the god who saved her, the baby girl grew into a beautiful woman. The story eventually ends with her marriage to a handsome chief of the area. Today, the cliff trail to Nuʻalolo ʻĀina and the swinging ladder have vanished, the victims of age and erosion, but their memory is perpetuated in the name of the point, Alapiʻi, meaning "path (of) ascension." Alapiʻi also means "ladder."

The most spectacular feature at Nuʻalolo Kai Beach is the extensive reef flat that fans seaward from the eastern point of the bay. At its widest point, it extends 600 feet from the beach. A deep channel along the western reef slope penetrates to the beach. With outer depths of 25 feet, the channel provides an excellent leeward anchorage for large boats and allows smaller boats to go directly ashore. The ocean bottom in the main channel consists of a maze of smaller sand channels separated by narrow ridges of limestone and scattered limestone pinnacles. During periods of calm seas, particularly during the summer, the channel offers excellent opportunities for snorkeling and scuba diving. Many commercial tour boats bring their groups here to snorkel and to picnic onshore.

Nuʻalolo Reef is one of the most unusual reefs in the major Hawaiian Islands. Although many other reefs are much more extensive, it is among the best examples in Hawaiʻi of an actively growing, pristine fringing reef. Its location in such a remote site has allowed it to develop without degradation resulting from stream run-off, agricultural development, modern human habitation, or any of the other problems that now plague so many Hawaiian reefs. Nuʻalolo Reef supports virtually every common shallow-water reef coral in Hawaiʻi, in addition to many varieties of seaweed, a very large community of invertebrates, and more than fifty species of fish. The inner reef flat is an important "nursery" for many juvenile reef fish, but is deep enough at high tide to attract large schools of foraging adults. Octopus and shells are also seen in many cracks and crevices. With its great diversity of sea life, Nuʻalolo Reef once provided sustenance for native Hawaiians. Today, it is visited primarily by snorkelers, and on occasion by local fishermen.

The seaward perimeter of the reef is a massive buttress built up by coralline algae. The buttress serves as a barrier between the body of the reef and the open ocean. In many areas, its upper edge is an elevated ridge that is exposed at low tide. The outer reef flat is a smooth limestone surface perforated by thousands of small holes and cracks. High surf striking the reef has undercut the platform, allowing the water below the flat to push up through the holes and cracks. When an incoming wave flows along the reef at low tide, water bubbles up and gurgles in every single perforation. Thousands of minature blow holes perform in sequence immediately in front of the incoming wave and retreat as the white water washes by, a phenomenom that is fascinating to watch.

A second, smaller reef fronts the Nuʻalolo coastal flat to the west of the boat channel. It is comprised of young expanding apron reefs bordering the shoreline almost to Mākuaiki Point. They are characterized by partially interconnected limestone mounds, pinnacles, coral heads, and a series of large surge channels, harboring many kinds of sea life.

Nuʻalolo Kai Beach is a long, narrow beach that begins in the lee of Alapiʻi Point. Its foreshore slopes steeply to the vegetation line, a clear indication that high surf sweeps over the reef and strikes the shore with force. Beachrock lines much of the sand at the water's edge. Facilities in the backshore include portable toilets, a roofed picnic shelter, and two landing markers to guide boats into the channel. As the beach progresses west beyond the protection of Nu'alolo Reef, the shoreline becomes rocky, a mixture of pebbles, boulders, and patches of sand.

During the winter and spring, when high surf assaults the entire Nā Pali coast, powerful waves break across the bay, precluding all boat landings. The surf causes dangerous rip currents to form within the bay and strong longshore currents beyond the surfline. A particularly powerful rip current runs out to sea through the channel to the beach.

Miloli'i Beach

The first of the valleys beyond Polihale is Miloli'i, a narrow valley with steep sides. It had a good stream, and taro was raised in many *lo'i,* some of which had facings of stone built up 8 feet from ground level. There must have been a sizable population, for the names of six temples or shrines were recorded by Francis Gay, who surveyed this region.

Native Planters in Old Hawaii
Handy, Handy, and Pukui, 1972

Miloli'i is the westernmost of the wilderness beaches in Nā Pali Coast State Park. It is located just around Mākuaiki Point from Nu'alolo and approximately 4 miles from the western end of the beach at Polihale State Park. It is accessible only by boat. The Miloli'i shoreline is a narrow coastal flat that is bounded by steep sea cliffs. The coastal flat, covering an area one mile long and 500 feet wide, was once the site of a small Hawaiian fishing village. Miloli'i Valley, opening onto the western end of the coastal flat, once supported a larger Hawaiian settlement, complete with a public school.

By the turn of the twentieth century, the Hawaiian families that had inhabited Miloli'i were gone, having left their remote shoreline and valley homes to live in more populous parts of the island. Today, only the ruins of their habitation sites and agricultural terraces still remain.

Miloli'i Beach, a long, beautiful stretch of sand, wraps around a gently curving point and ends at Keawanui, where a boulder beach begins. The foreshore is steep, the result of seasonal high surf that strikes the Nā

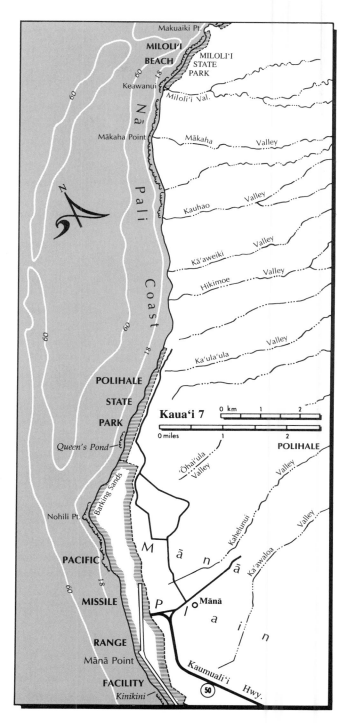

47

Pali coastline. The waves also move the sand offshore and onshore, causing marked seasonal changes in the beach. Sand erosion is common during the winter and spring, the high surf season, whereas sand usually accretes during the summer.

A large, well-developed fringing reef fronts much of the Miloli'i shoreline. At its widest point, the reef extends 250 feet offshore. Nearshore sections of the reef are shallow and emerge at low tide. Mud covers a portion of the inner reef where an intermittent stream drains into the ocean. The Miloli'i reef supports many common shallow-water corals, a wide variety of seaweeds, a large community of invertebrates, and more than thirty species of fish. Green sea turtles are frequently seen foraging on and around the reef flat. Snorkeling opportunities are excellent during periods of calm seas. Local fishermen frequent the area to spear and net fish. A narrow boat channel blasted out of the reef provides access to the beach from the ocean.

Miloli'i Beach is one of the best shelling beaches in Hawai'i. Cowries, cones, and several varieties of Ni'ihau shells are common, particularly during the winter months immediately after periods of high surf. Beachcombers also find many other treasures along the debris line, including Japanese fishing floats made of hand-blown glass, popularly known as glass balls. Facilities located in the vegetated sand dunes in the backshore include portable toilets, roofed picnic shelters, a cabin for park personnel, and two landing markers to guide boats into the channel.

During the winter and spring, powerful waves breaking along the entire length of Miloli'i Beach preclude all boat landings. The surf creates dangerous rip currents and strong longshore currents beyond the surfline. A particularly powerful rip current runs out to sea through the narrow channel to the beach. Periods of high surf also create a surfing break on the outer edge of the reef flat, but surfing here is for experts only.

POLIHALE STATE PARK. One of the longest continuous sand beaches in Hawai'i begins at Polihale State Park and ends 15 miles away in Kekaha. Polihale, also one of the widest beaches in the state, is backed by extensive sand dunes, some over 100 feet above sea level. Two visitors appear to be crossing a desert here at the west end of the beach.

Polihale State Park

'Ike 'ike one kani a o Nohili
Me ka pāpale a o Polihale.

Widely known are the sounding sands of Nohili
At the crest of Polihale.

"Nohili"
Traditional song

One of the longest continuous sand beaches in Hawai'i begins at Polihale State Park, winds its way around the Mānā Coastal Plain, and ends 15 miles away in Kekaha. Polihale State Park, a 140-acre park, borders the first 2.25 miles at the northwestern end of the beach.

Polihale Beach averages over 300 feet in width during the summer. It is slightly narrower during the winter when high surf erodes the foreshore. The backshore consists of massive sand dunes which are 50 to 100 feet high at Nohili Point. In the midst of this extensive sand dune complex are Hawai'i's famous Barking Sands. The Hawaiians called them Keonekani o Nohili, "The Sounding Sands of Nohili." This phrase, once a well-known saying that was representative of Kaua'i, appears often in traditional songs and chants that mention the special features of the individual islands.

To English speakers early on, the noises emitted by the sands when they were agitated sounded like the woofing or barking of a dog. In 1875 the Barking Sands were described in a letter (published in *The Islander*) from W. R. Frink of Honolulu to the California Academy of Sciences:

> If you slap two handfuls of the sand together, a sound is produced like the hooting of an owl. If a person kneels on the steep incline, and then, with the two hands extended and grasping as much sand as possible, slides rapidly down, carrying all the sand he can, the sound accumulates till it is like distant thunder. But the greatest sound we produced was by having one native lie upon his belly, and another take him by the feet and drag him rapidly down the incline. With this experiment the sound was terrific, and could have been heard many yards away.

Frink also sent a sample of sand with his letter. Dr. James Blake of the California Academy of Sciences investigated the sample and offered these observations:

The grains are all, more or less, perforated with small holes, mostly terminating in blind cavities, which are frequently enlarged in the interior, communicating with the surface by a small opening. The structure of the grains explains the reason why sounds are emitted when they are set in motion. The mutual friction causes vibrations in their substance and consequently in the sides of the cavities; and, these vibrations being communicated to the air in the cavities, the result is sound. There are, in fact, millions upon millions of resonant cavities, each giving out a sound which may well acquire a great volume, and even resemble a peal of thunder. The sand must be dry, however, in order to produce sound; for, when the cavities are filled with water, the grains are incapable of originating vibrations.

Barking sands, or singing sands as other observers have called them, have been documented in other parts of the world, notably in the Sinai Desert in Egypt, in the Gobi Desert in Mongolia, in the Atacama Desert in Chile, and in the Empty Quarter in Saudi Arabia. Hawaiian tradition refers to two other barking sand sites, one at 'Ohikilolo on O'ahu and one at Kaluakahua on Ni'ihau, both of which are also called *keonekani*, "the sounding sands."

Polihale marks the end of the road at the western edge of the Nā Pali sea cliffs, much as Hā'ena marks the end of the road at the eastern edge. Polihale State Park offers amenities such as restrooms, showers, picnic pavilions, and camping areas, but beachgoers should be aware that there are no lifeguards at this remote, wilderness site. High surf, particularly during the winter and spring, generates dangerous water conditions that have caused many drownings and near-drownings. Powerful rip currents run along the water's edge where the ocean bottom often drops sharply to overhead depths. These currents have caught many unsuspecting swimmers and pulled them out to sea. High surf often sweeps up to the base of the sand dunes, covering the entire beach. Beachcombers walking along the shore have been trapped in the backwash and carried into the ocean. Be extremely cautious on the beach during any period of high surf, and unless you are an expert in Hawaiian surf, do not go swimming.

An extensive sand bar extends offshore of the beach several hundred yards into the ocean. Surf breaking on the sand bar occasionally attracts surfers and bodyboarders, but the waves are often shifty and unpredictable. This surfing site is usually used only during periods of smaller surf. A more popular and predictable surfing site called Rocket Reef is located near the southwest end of the park, immediately offshore of the rocket launching pad at the Pacific Missile Range Facility.

The safest swimming site at Polihale State Park is a small, protected inlet called Queen's Pond. This shallow, sand-bottomed pond is situated in a small apron reef adjoining the beach. The reef protects the pond from normal wave action and longshore currents. During periods of calm seas, it is a favorite site for families with children. During periods of high surf, however, waves sweep over the reef and into the pond, creating a strong rip current. The rip current runs through an opening in the southern margin of the reef and empties into the deeper ocean beyond. Queens Pond is also a popular windsurfing and wave jumping site during periods of strong west and northwest winds. Boardsailors ride the breaks on the southern side of the pond.

According to an account by Dorothy Blackman in a 1936 issue of *Paradise of the Pacific* magazine, Queens Pond, or Queens Bath, was named for a queen of Kaua'i who bathed there. Her name was Leilani. Enchanted by her beauty, Kalanikaula, a chief from O'ahu, asked for her hand in marriage, but chief Kana of Kaua'i refused his request. A battle between the armies of the two chiefs took place at Nohili and left many dead on the sand dunes, including Kana. Distraught by the deaths caused by the fighting, Leilani consumed a magic potion and turned into a seabird. From that time on, the sands near her pond have emitted a variety of sounds commemorating the battle: thunder, groans of pain, and the rustling of women's skirts.

Queens Pond is located approximately midway along the shoreline fronting the beach park. To approach it, turn south on the main park access road at the fork marked by two monkeypod trees, and proceed 0.2 mile. An access road leads up on to the dunes and overlooks the pond. Drivers need to be very cautious in this area. The wind-blown sand constantly shifts on the access roads on the dunes, making drifts that are often deep enough to stall a car.

Polihale State Park is reached by driving to the end of Kaumuali'i Highway at Māna and following the signs that direct the public through the sugar cane fields. The distance along the cane haul roads from the highway to the park is 5 miles.

Pacific Missile Range Facility

The Sandia Corporation fired its first 100-mile-high weather rocket from Barking Sands last night after more than a week of delay and frustration. Project manager J. J. Miller said the fluorescent-trail wind measuring device was "completely successful and even more spectacular than I expected."

Last night's rocket, launched at about 8:30, could be seen rising to about 500,000 feet from many parts of the island. Mr. Miller said the vapor trail extended downward from about 100 miles to 50 miles, and stretched to the west between 49 and 55 miles.

The Garden Island
February 5, 1964

The Pacific Missile Range Facility, a multipurpose naval installation, is located on the shoreline of the Māna Coastal Plain. Many local residents simply call the site PMR. The Pacific Missile Range Facility is one of the foremost centers in the world for the detection of aircraft or vessels in the Pacific. With its highly sophisticated computers and electronic equipment, the facility can detect underwater activities and estimate the depth, range, and bearing of a ship, a submarine, or any other marine vessel. Listening devices on the ocean floor in the Underwater Range offshore of the facility can pinpoint within 10 to 15 feet a vessel's location within an area of 1,000 square miles. Radar units on base, at Mākaha Ridge and at Kōke'e, allow the detection of surface ships and aircraft over 17,000 square miles of ocean. The Pacific Missile Range Facility conducts combat training exercises using its extensive resources. All of the actions and reactions of the units involved are recorded on the facility's computers and can be replayed immediately in a screening room.

Radio Station WWVH is also located within the facility. This high-frequency station is one of two in the United States operated by the U.S. Department of Commerce. It broadcasts time signals to trans-Pacific ships and aircraft.

The range employs 130 military personnel, 80 govern-

PACIFIC MISSILE RANGE FACILITY. A gentle shorebreak washes onshore at Majors Bay in the Pacific Missile Range Facility. During periods of high surf, wave heights in the bay often reach 10 to 15 feet. The high eastern sea cliffs of Niʻihau are clearly visible across Kaulakahi Channel as is Lehua Island slightly to the north.

ment service workers, 460 employees of the civilian contractor who does most of the maintenance and technical work, and 50 employees of several other defense support businesses. This large work force makes the Pacific Range Missile Facility one of Kauaʻi's leading employers and an important part of the island's economy.

One of the most impressive aspects of the facility for the people of Kauaʻi has been its very positive, long-term interaction with the civilian community. Out of all of the shoreline military installations in the islands, the Pacific Range Missile Facility provides one of the best examples of how a good-neighbor policy can be established and implemented. The facility is active in community affairs and has established a scholarship program for children from the civilian community. Surf casters,

throw-net fishermen, surfers, windsurfers, and other beachgoers are regularly allowed to cross the base to get to the beach. Visitors need only to check in at the security desk with a valid driver's license, a current no-fault insurance card, and record of a current safety check. Certain areas are periodically off-limits during flight operations or during other scheduled exercises. All of these considerations by the military for the civilian community have resulted in an excellent relationship between the two for many years.

The beach fronting the facility is a continuation of the long, wide beach that begins at Polihale, wraps around the Mānā Coastal Plain, and ends at Kekaha. The shoreline at Nohili Point and south of it is fronted by long, massive sections of beachrock, offering excellent opportunities for shoreline fishing and throw-netting. Surfers frequent a break on the north side of the point called Rockets or Rocket Reef. The break is located offshore of the rocket launching pad where rocket firings have taken place since 1964 to measure high altitude winds in Hawai'i and to gather other scientific information.

Three other important surfing sites are located offshore of the facility: Kinikini at the south end of the runway, Majors Bay at Recreation Area #3, and Family Housing at the on-base family housing area. Of the three sites, Majors Bay is most used and is rarely closed to the public. Majors Bay and Kinikini are also important windsurfing sites.

Majors Bay was named for the base's former commanders, who held the rank of major and occupied the house on the northern point of the bay. The Majors Bay surfing site is offshore of the house which today is used as transient quarters for visiting dignitaries. A new home for the base commanders, along with a family housing complex, was constructed in the mid-1970s.

The beach fronting the Pacific Missile Range Facility is exposed to the open ocean. High surf, particularly during the winter and spring, generates dangerous water conditions, including pounding shorebreaks, strong backwashes, and powerful rip currents. Fringing reefs adjoin the shoreline in two areas, Nohili and Mānā

points, but they do not offer any protection to the shoreline for swimming. During these periods of high surf, in-water activities are limited to experts only.

The Pacific Missile Range Facility is located at Mānā Point near the western end of Kaumuali'i Highway.

Kekaha Beach Park

Kekaha Sugar Co. had its beginnngs in 1878, although the site of the plantation was used for growing cane years before by Valdemar Knudsen, who arrived in the district in 1856, leased land from the government and erected a thatched house.

[Knudsen's son] Eric A. Knudsen recalls that the land which is now covered with sugar cane was once under water, forming a marsh and inland waterway. There were large villages of Hawaiians living at Barking Sands, and rows of Hawaiian thatched houses along the foothills bordering the water. The Hawaiians traveled by canoe from Mana to Waimea through this inland waterway.

Honolulu Star-Bulletin
May 11, 1935

Kekaha Beach Park lies near the end of the 15-mile-long beach that stretches along the Mānā Coastal Plain from Polihale southward to Kekaha. The portion of the beach between the Pacific Missile Range Facility and the beach park includes several miles of shoreline winding

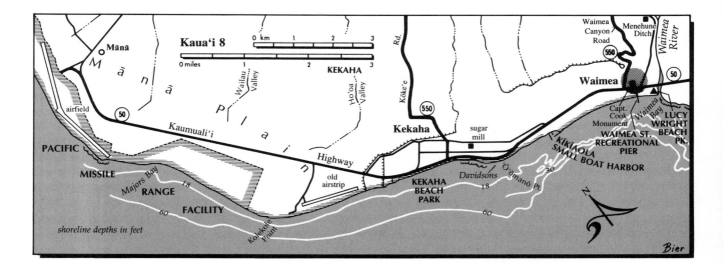

around Kokole Point. The lands between Kaumuali'i Highway and the beach are used primarily for agriculture. Non-agricultural uses include a county landfill, a rifle range, and an abandoned landing strip that was leased from the state for some years as the Mānā Drag Strip. Although there are no public rights-of-way to this shoreline, it is visited regularly by fishermen, surfers, joggers, and beachcombers. Most of them gain access either by driving over a number of unmarked dirt roads to the old landing strip or simply by following the beach from Kekaha Beach Park. To reach the old landing strip, turn off Kaumuali'i Highway at Bridge No. 3.

Surfers probably make up the largest group of ocean users at Kokole Point. Some of the surfing sites they frequent are Rifle Range, Targets, and Whispering Sands. Bodyboarders and bodysurfers occasionally ride these breaks. High surf, particularly during the winter and spring, generates very powerful rip currents and longshore currents along this shoreline. Anyone entering the water stands an excellent chance of being dragged along the beach through the surf for several hundred yards in a matter of minutes. The pounding shorebreak produces waves that are very steep and dangerous. These waves, breaking over the extensive sand bars that parallel the beach, almost routinely snap surfboards in half. If you are not an expert in Hawaiian surf, do not swim here during periods of high surf.

Kekaha Beach Park is located on Kaumuali'i Highway at the western end of Kekaha town. The improved portion of the beach park, including all of its facilities, are located across the road from the beach.

For many years shoreline erosion was a major problem here. As a result of the erosion, more than 16 acres of sand beach were lost and the coastal highway was damaged. The Army Corps of Engineers took corrective action in 1980, constructing a seawall to protect the highway.

Kekaha Beach attracts a variety of beachgoers, including fishermen and swimmers, as well as bodyboarders and surfers who enjoy the surfing sites immediately west of the beach park—Inters, First Ditch, and Second Ditch. Inters is located offshore of the intersection of Kaumuali'i Highway and Akialoa Street, while First Ditch and Second Ditch are located in front of two drainage ditches. These popular shorebreak sites are

very dangerous during periods of high surf, particularly during the winter and spring, when the waves generate powerful rip currents and longshore currents. No one who is not an expert in Hawaiian surf should swim here during periods of high surf.

Surfers also ride a break at the southern end of Kekaha Beach called Davidsons. It was named after James Douglas Davidson, a former long-time resident of the area. Davidson came to Kaua'i in 1919 and was employed by Kekaha Sugar Company. In 1922, he built a two-story house across the road from the beach and lived there until his death in 1949. The names Davidsons Beach and Davidsons Point fronting his home became popular shortly after his death. The surfing site at 'Ō'ōmanō Point, or Davidsons Point, breaks over a shallow apron reef adjoining the beach.

Kīkīaola Small Boat Harbor

Rather than still another resolution asking the state or nation to do something about the beach erosion at Kekaha, Councilwoman Rose Ono Shaw suggests dynamiting the Kikiaola Small Boat Harbor.

"I have talked to the people, the 'Ohana of Kekaha," Mrs. Shaw said, " and they say if the little harbor in Kekaha is blown up, the beach will be restored."

She explained there had been no problems before the installation of Kikiaola Harbor, which folks feel has caused the change in currents which ate away the beach. Eight or nine years ago there was a 100 yard beach, now the waves break over the road.

The Garden Island
November 19, 1976

One of the longest continuous sand beaches in Hawai'i begins at Polihale State Park, winds its way around the Mānā Coastal Plain, and ends 15 miles away at Kīkīaola Small Boat Harbor in Kekaha. Although the beach adjoining the harbor is shallow and sandy, it is infrequently used for swimming. Beachgoers find the beach unappealing because of the large amount of silt in the sand, from Davidson Point to the harbor.

The state of Hawai'i built Kīkīaola Small Boat Harbor in 1959 to provide an alternative facility for the boaters of West Kaua'i. Prior to the harbor's construction, the nearest facility was Port Allen, over 8 miles away. While the initial idea for a harbor was sound, the site has been plagued by a number of problems. The two original breakwaters proved inadequate to control the surge within the harbor basin, particularly during periods of high surf. In 1964, two stub breakwaters and a short inner breakwater were added to mitigate the problem. The harbor basin is also subject to sand accretion problems, which have necessitated dredging of the harbor bottom several times. And finally, high surf on the reefs offshore of the harbor makes entry and exit precarious.

In spite of the problems, the harbor is used regularly by local boaters. Facilities include restrooms, drinking water, parking for automobiles and trailers, a marina, a paved launching ramp, and a wharf of marginal utility. The shore area is visited primarily by fishermen, beachcombers, and picnickers.

Waimea State Recreation Pier

Dominador "Domi" Acain says he and his friends do not chase women anymore. They do not gamble and they do not drink. In fact, says the 64-year-old Acain, the only enjoyment he and his friends, Takeo Matsumoto, Uedo Fukumoto and Tomo Kawada, seem to get out of life is sitting with their fishing poles in the hot sun on Waimea Pier. Now even that small pleasure appears to be in jeopardy.

State game wardens have come to the pier and warned Acain and his friends against taking the undersized mullet that swim in the muddy waters beneath the pier.

"How much they going to catch?" asks Kawada, 75, pointing to the line of retired Japanese and Filipino plantation workers sitting with their fishing poles and their coolers at the edge of the pier. The women wear straw field hats and white scarves against the late afternoon sun. The men wear baseball caps.

"The netters come in here with small eye mesh net and take everything, and they [the state game wardens] don't do a thing, but they see us out here trying to catch one or two fish and they say they are going to give us a ticket. I don't like breaking the law, but what we going to do? If we don't catch the small ones, we don't catch nothing."

Kawada's concerns are echoed by others on Kauai and throughout the state as scientists report the severe decline (and in some cases the collapse) of Hawaii's nearshore fisheries. Kauai's problems are a microcosm of a state-wide fish scarcity that is provoking frustration and, occasionally, violent confrontations among Hawaii's fishermen.

Honolulu magazine
June 1988

Waimea State Recreation Pier is situated on the beach fronting the town of Waimea. It is located at the end of Moana Road, a short residential street that intersects Kaumuali'i Highway. The pier, an abandoned boat landing, attracts many local fishing enthusiasts. Commonly caught fish include mullet, *papi'o,* and āholehole, all of which inhabit the nearby lower estuarine reaches of Waimea River.

Regulations established by the Department of Land and Natural Resources state that no one shall use a spear, trap, throw net, or any other type of net within 50 yards of the pier. Information on other fishing restrictions at the site may be obtained by contacting the Department of Land and Natural Resources office in Līhu'e.

The pier adjoins the detrital sand beach that begins at Kīkīaola Small Boat Harbor and ends at Waimea River. The nearshore bottom on either side of the pier is sandy, but the water is usually dirty from soil carried into the ocean by the river, which discourages swimmers. Occasional high surf causes dangerous water conditions, particularly a pounding shorebreak, a strong backwash, and powerful rip currents. Park facilities include a paved parking lot, restrooms, and a picnic area.

Lucy Wright Beach Park

By the end of the day the *Resolution* and the *Discovery* were close to the village of Waimea, a cluster of about sixty huts near the beach and another forty or so farther inland. The ships spent the night standing off the coast, and next morning some natives nerved themselves to come aboard. It was an overwhelming experience for them. "Their eyes," wrote Cook, "were continually flying from object to object, the wildness of their looks and actions fully express'd their surprise and astonishment, at the several new objects before them and evinced that they never had been on board of a ship before."

Shoal of Time
Daws, 1968

LUCY WRIGHT BEACH PARK. The beach fronting Lucy Wright Beach Park and the rest of Waimea town is dark and strewn with litter, the result of soil and debris discharged into the ocean by Waimea River. The murky nearshore waters rarely attract swimmers, but surfers often ride the waves offshore.

Lucy Wright Beach Park, located on the western bank of the Waimea River, was named in honor of the first native Hawaiian school teacher at Waimea School. Lucy Kapahu Aukai Wright, born August 20, 1873, in Anahola, taught for one year at Anahola, for two years at Kapa'a, and then for thirty-five years at Waimea. She was a member of Waimea Hawaiian Church and of many civic organizations, and was a beloved member of the community. She died on August 2, 1931, and is buried in the graveyard at Waimea Foreign Church. The park that is named in her honor is also the site where Captain James Cook first came ashore in the Hawaiian Islands in January 1778. Prior to Cook's discovery of the islands, Hawai'i had been unknown to the Western world.

Facilities at the park include restrooms, showers, and parking. The detrital beach sand here is dark and the nearshore waters are murky from soil that is brought downstream by the river. While the beach and the ocean are generally unappealing to sunbathers and swimmers, surfers occasionally ride the shorebreak that forms offshore the river mouth. The site breaks best on a south swell, but will also break on a west or northwest swell. High surf causes dangerous water conditions, particularly a pounding shorebreak and powerful rip currents.

During the summer the amount of water in the river drops, and a sand bar forms across the river mouth. Local outrigger canoe paddlers take advantage of these conditions and practice in the river. The estuary extends nearly 2 miles upstream, affording considerable inland access for shallow-draft boats such as the canoes. The river and the adjoining beach are also popular with pole and throw-net fishermen.

On the east bank of the Waimea River directly across from Lucy Wright Beach Park are the ruins of a Russian fort built between 1815 and 1817 during an alliance between the Russian-American Company and King Kaumuali'i of Kaua'i. The Russians, represented by a German named Georg Anton Scheffer, designed the fort and directed the large Hawaiian work force that constructed its walls. Russian occupation of the fort ended abruptly in 1817 when the Russians were expelled from Hawai'i by King Kamehameha I. Hawaiian soldiers then occupied the structure until 1864 when it was deactivated by order of the Hawaiian government.

Today the fort is a 17.3-acre state park known as Russian Fort Elizabeth State Historical Park. It is marked by a sign on Kaumuali'i Highway.

Pākalā Beach

At Pakala, the neighborhood of many Hawaiians, one house appears to be smashed [by Hurricane 'Iwa]. The picnic park is being bulldozed. Community efforts to help neighbors rebuild house and garden is obvious in the bustle on the muddy roads.

Near Pakala, the sturdy metal landing boat that takes Hawaiians to and from Niihau is snug in its denuded harbor, ready for a trip, Hawaiians say, at the end of the week.

The Garden Island
November 26, 1982

Pākalā is one of Kaua'i's most famous beaches. Its fame resides not in the beach itself, but in the surfing waves offshore. The surfing break is known either as Pākalā or Infinity, or the plurals of both—Pākalās or Infinities. Of the four options, the most commonly used name is Infinities.

Infinities fronts Pākalā Village, a plantation camp on the beach located 2 miles east of the mouth of Waimea River. The village and the lands surrounding it are part of the Gay and Robinson sugar plantation, and several members of the Robinson family have shoreline homes next to the village. The name Infinity was given to the surfing site in 1962 by Randy Weir, a member of one of the Robinson families that has a home there on the beach. Beginning in 1962 Randy, then a teenaged surfer from Kailua High School on O'ahu, began spending his summers surfing the waves offshore the family's Kaua'i home. He felt that riding the extremely long, seemingly endless Pākalā waves was like surfing into infinity. He

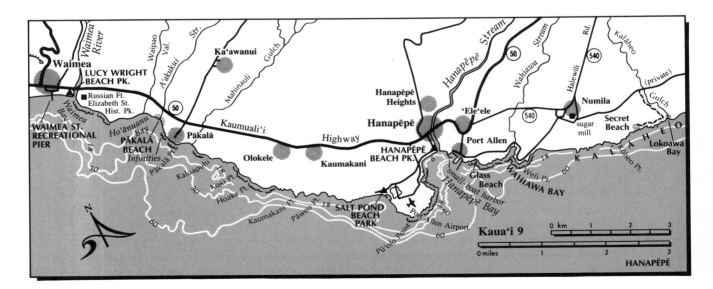

56

PākalĀ. The wide, shallow reef fronting Pākalā Village is the site of Infinities, one of the most famous surfing breaks in Hawai'i. During the summer months waves reach heights of 10 to 12 feet and offer one of the longest left slides in Hawaiian waters. Pākalā Village, a largely Hawaiian community, houses many families from Ni'ihau.

coined the name Infinity, and it was soon picked up by the Hawaiian surfing community.

Infinities is one of the best summer surfing sites in Hawai'i. The waves form on the western end of an extensive, shallow fringing reef fronting Pākalā Village. Reef breaks of this type are common throughout the islands, but the Pākalā reef has the exact edge and slope to create the perfect wave. Summer swells striking the gently curving reef are transformed into beautifully shaped left-slide waves. Waves heights of 6 feet or greater allow surfers to ride from offshore Pākalā Vil-

lage all the way to the mouth of A'akukui Stream, one of the longest rides in Hawai'i. The name Infinities is certainly appropriate.

Surfers also ride several other breaks offshore Pākalā Point along the eastern edge of the reef. These breaks also offer excellent, well-formed waves, but the rides are much shorter. The reef here is quite shallow, so surfers use these sites generally only at high tide.

Infinities is also well known for its "chocolate walls," a reference to the ever-present dirty water at Pākalā Point. A stream on the east side of the village continually discharges muddy water into the ocean, and the prevailing current picks it up and carries it across the reef and through the surfing site. Shark sightings in the murky water are common.

The unmarked public right-of-way to Infinities is located at the A'akukui Stream Bridge, 1.4 miles east of Waimea River. Parking is available on either side of the road. For many years this 150-yard path was not a public right-of-way and was the scene of many arrests for trespassing. The only way to reach Infinities besides using this access is to follow the beach from Waimea River, a very long walk. When Hawai'i's surfers first started to come to the area in the 1960s, they naturally opted for the shorter distance, but in so doing started a running battle between themselves and the landowner, the Gay and Robinson plantation. The plantation management was determined that no one should cross the cattle pasture without their permission, and in keeping with this policy they made numerous citizen's arrests of surfers crossing their property. Within two months during the summer of 1968 more than 30 people were arrested and fined for trespassing. The situation was finally resolved in the 1970s when the county stepped in and negotiated public use of the right-of-way.

The Makaweli shoreline between Pākalā Village and Salt Pond Beach Park is mostly rocky with a few narrow stretches of sand and several small pocket beaches. The largest concentration of sand is at Kaluapuhi. Much of the nearshore ocean bottom fronting the beaches is shallow and rocky, and the water is often murky. The agricultural lands along this shoreline are owned by the Gay and Robinson plantation and include the Olokele Mill. There is no public access.

Salt Pond Beach Park

He ālialia pa'akai, he ālialia manu, nā ālialia o nā waipuna hu'ihu'i.

It is a salt bed, a salt bed for birds, salt encrusted places with cool springs.

Traditional saying
Hawaiian Dictionary

The production of rock salt by evaporating seawater is an ancient Hawaiian process that is still practiced near Salt Pond Beach Park. The ponds at the park are the only ones in the Hawaiian Islands that are still in use; all of the other traditional sites are now abandoned. Here, the evaporation pans and several large ponds are located on a natural flat near the beach.

Salt-making is a summer-time project whose success is dependent upon extended periods of dry weather and hot sun. Rain during the winter months dilutes or completely dissolves the drying salt. In May the shallow wells, or *puna,* are cleaned of the debris that has accumulated in the off-season. These wells are holding tanks that are used to increase the salinity of natural sea water. As the water level in them drops from evaporation, more ocean water is pumped into them. Then the water in the *puna* is transferred to a set of shallower holding tanks called *waikū* where, in the same way, the salt concentration is made even greater. And finally, water from the *waikū* is pumped into *ālia,* or shallow pans, where it is allowed to evaporate completely.

After two or three days, the salt has crystalized. It is pushed with a wooden rake into a mound in the center of the bed or into the highest corner. There it is allowed to drain briefly. Then it is removed from the bed and stored where it can drain completely dry. The final product is bagged and used as needed.

A common addition to the finished product, *pa'akai,* is *'alaea,* commonly shortened in speech to *'alae. 'Alaea,* a red, water-soluble, colloidal clay, colors the salt red. *'Alaea* is also traditionally valued as a medicine, a dye, and a component in the mixtures used at ritual purification ceremonies. Because it is so highly prized, the locations of *'alaea* deposits are often closely guarded secrets.

Most of the salt ponds in the complex at Salt Pond Beach Park are supervised by Hui Hana Pa'akai, an organization whose members are permitted by the state to manufacture salt there. Many of the group's members have been working these beds since they were children, continuing a tradition that was practiced by the generations that preceded them, and using a method that has changed little since ancient times.

Salt Pond Beach Park lies between two rocky points. A natural ridge of rock runs between the two points, creating a large ponded area bordered by a crescent sand beach. The ridge is broken in many places, allowing the ocean to circulate freely inshore. This partially protected beach attracts many families with children. Swimming conditions are normally safe except during periods of high surf when rip currents form in several of the channels through the natural ridge offshore.

Salt Pond Beach Park is a popular surfing and windsurfing site. Surfers ride waves at several sites offshore, and the constant prevailing winds attract many windsurfers. During periods of calm seas scuba divers and spear fishermen frequent the wide expanse of the reef offshore.

Facilities in the park include a lifeguard tower, picnic pavilions, restrooms, showers, paved parking, and a camping area. The park is located west of Hanapēpē in the lee of Puʻolo Point. Port Allen Airport, formerly known as Burns Field, is located on the point. It is a landing site for small airplanes and helicopters.

Hanapēpē Beach Park

Two miles west of Wahiawa, and seven miles from Koloa, are the valley and falls of Hanapepe. These are remarkable among the scenery of the Hawaiian Islands. The banks are precipitous; from hundreds to thousands of feet high, the brink comes unheralded on the startled observer, who finds it impossible to descend, except by a few passes. Near the sea the valley widens, and the barrier walls decrease in height, exhibiting masses of red columnar lava. Here, close by the ocean, under the cocoanut trees, by the mouth of the stream that runs down the valley, are the homes of the natives, whose patches of taro and bananas line the banks above.

Tourist's Guide through Hawaii
Whitney, 1890

Hanapēpē Beach Park is located at the western end of Hanapēpē Bay. The waters fronting the small park are very murky due to the large amounts of sediment discharged by nearby Hanapēpē Stream. The seaward edge of the park is a boulder retaining wall, but a dark detrital sand beach adjoins the mouth of river. For many years shoreline erosion has been a problem here. Local residents attribute the loss of beach sand to the alteration of the shoreline with facilities to accommodate commercial and recreational boating.

Surfers occasionally ride a small shorebreak near the beach. Fishing and crabbing are more common pastimes, particularly in the river estuary. The bay is a breeding site for hammerhead sharks, and shoreline fishermen regularly net and hook juvenile hammerheads.

Facilities in the park include pavilions, restrooms, showers, and parking.

Port Allen

Port Allen is situated in Hanapepe Bay on the southern coast of Kauai, not far from the spot where Capt. Cook landed and where, almost 40 years later, the hopeful Russians built their fort. It lies about 20 nautical miles from Nawiliwili and 118 from Honolulu. The bay is about half a mile wide. Its shores are low, rocky bluffs except at its head, where there is a sandy beach.

The Ports of Hawaii
Stroup, 1950

Port Allen lies in the eastern corner of Hanapēpē Bay. The harbor is Kauaʻi's second major commercial deepwater port, after Nāwiliwili on the eastern coast of the island. Port Allen was named for Samuel C. Allen, a prominent businessman who, at the turn of the century, provided a substantial amount of money to improve ʻEleʻele Landing, the port's former name. Allen was a partner in Allen and Robinson, a chandlery and lumber business on the Honolulu waterfront. He had hoped to develop the landing into Kauaʻi's principal port, but its distance from Oʻahu and Honolulu Harbor eventually proved to be too great an obstacle. In April 1909 the Kauaʻi Railway Company, the owner of the terminal, renamed it in honor of Allen. Congress authorized the construction of the breakwater and the dredging of the entrance channel and turning basin in 1935. Additional dredging enlarged the turning basin to its present size in 1948.

Adjoining the Port Allen wharf complex is the Port Allen Small Boat Harbor, the major small-boat harbor on Kauaʻi's western side. Both recreational and commercial boaters make extensive use of its facilities, which include slips for mooring, a loading dock, a launching ramp, restrooms, and parking for trucks and trailers. The harbor facilities, completely destroyed in

1982 by Hurricane 'Iwa, were rebuilt by the state in 1985 in a 2.7-million-dollar project.

The waters of Port Allen and Hanapēpē Bay are murky and not inviting for activities other than boating, crabbing, fishing, and occasionally surfing. However, to the east of the Chevron fuel tank farm there is a small pocket beach that is a beachcomber's delight. The entire beach is covered with beach glass. Some local residents believe that the ocean currents transport the glass from a shoreline dump nearby, but whatever its source, it is plentiful. Some people call the site Glass Beach.

Wahiawa Bay

An excellent account of Wahiawa *ahupua'a* was given us in 1935 by Keahi Luahine, whose home this valley was in her childhood and youth. According to this *kama-'aina,* the taro terraces extended all the way down to the *muliwai* (inlet). *Palaha* was the variety of taro that grew best in Wahiawa. It had a dark stalk; and dark flesh which was round and pointed at the bottom, making purplish *poi.*

Native Planters in Old Hawaii
Handy, Handy, and Pukui, 1972

WAHIAWA. Accompanied by his dog, a fisherman sets up his sand spike and pole for shore casting in Wahiawa Bay. The large, sand-bottomed bay is deeply indented into the shoreline, offering excellent protection from the prevailing winds and currents. For this reason it is sometimes used by small boats as an anchorage.

Wahiawa is the name of a stream, a valley, a bay, and a beach. All of these sites fall within the land division, or *ahupua'a*, of Wahiawa and take their name from it. Although the name is spelled the same as the land division and town in central O'ahu, the two names have different pronounciations and therefore different meanings. The O'ahu name, spelled Wahiawā, with a macron on the last *a*, means "place of noise." The Kaua'i name, spelled without any diacritical marks, means "place [of the] milkfish."

One traditional story says that the Kaua'i name comes from a large stone basin where *awa*, or milkfish, were placed temporarily to keep them alive after they were caught. The site in the valley where the stone basin was located was called Wahiawa, the "place [where the] milkfish [were stored]." This stone and other legendary Hawaiian stones are located in nearby Kalāheo in Kukuiolono Park, the former home of Walter McBryde. McBryde, a member of an old Kaua'i family, feared that these culturally important stones would be lost as lands were cleared for development, so he gathered those he could find and placed them in his garden.

Wahiawa Bay is also identified as Ahulua Bay in some of the archaeological literature that documents sites in the area. The word *ahulua* means "two altars" and may indicate the number of temples that were once located on the bay.

Wahiawa Bay is a large, sand-bottomed bay that is lined on both sides with low sea cliffs. It is deeply indented into the shoreline, which gives it excellent protection from the prevailing winds and currents. For this reason, it is used as an anchorage by small boats in all except southerly, or *kona*, winds. A straight, moderately steep sand beach lines the head of the bay. The beach and the nearshore sand are mixed with silt, the result of runoff from Wahiawa Stream. The degraded condition of the stream and the bay dates back to the 1930s and the failure of an inland dam. The dam collapsed during its construction, inundating the bay with a massive flood of mud. The mud not only mixed in with the sand in the bay, but filled the Wahiawa Stream estuary which was formerly navigable in a small boat for about a quarter of a mile inland.

Although the beach and the bay still show signs of this mud flow, they are excellent for sunbathing, swimming, snorkeling, and fishing. The backshore is lined with shoreline vegetation including *milo*, ironwoods, and opiuma. Bougainvillea overhangs the sea cliffs that line the bay. Except for a little landscaping, the beach is undeveloped. There are no facilities. To reach the bay follow Highway 570 toward McBryde Mill (also known as Nūmila) and turn right on the cane road that leads to the shoreline. The McBryde Sugar Company controls the access road to the shoreline and reserves the right to close it to the public at any time.

Kalāheo

Aia ka makani la i Kauai, The winds of Kauai are:
He Aoao ko Hanapepe, The Aoao of Hanapepe,
He Unulau ko Wahiawa, The Unulau of Wahiawa,
He Kiuanu ko Kalaheo. The Kiuanu of Kalaheo.

Hawaiian Antiquities and Folklore
Fornander, 1918

The Kalāheo shoreline is predominantly sea cliffs. To the west of Kōheo Point several narrow strips of sand are located among the boulders at the base of the cliffs. These remote sites are visited only by throw-net and pole fishermen who hike down the cliffs to the tiny beaches below. To the east of Kōheo Point two small, accessible pocket sand beaches are found at the heads of two gulches. The first is in a narrow, unnamed gulch immediately west of Kalāheo Gulch and the second is in Kalāheo Gulch.

The first beach, known to some beachgoers as Secret Beach, is a large pocket of sand at the bottom of a narrow gulch. It is bordered by low lava points. The nearshore bottom is a moderately shallow shelf of flat rock. Small surf breaking over the shelf provides waves suitable for bodysurfing and bodyboarding. High surf generates dangerous water conditions, particularly a strong shorebreak and powerful rip currents.

The access road from the cane fields below Nūmila is steep and rutted, suitable only for vehicles with four-wheel drives.

The second beach, located in Kalāheo Gulch, is a large, flat pocket of sand fronted entirely by boulders. A small area has been cleared of rocks to create a wading area for children, but otherwise the site is not suit-

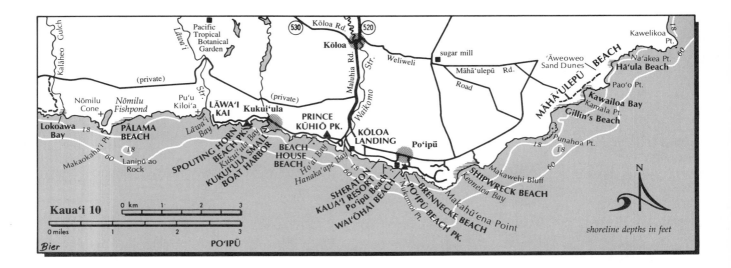

able for most in-water activities. The water inshore is murky from the mud brought by a small stream that empties into the ocean across the eastern end of the beach. A roofed picnic shelter sits in the backshore. The gulch and the access roads leading to it are on private property.

Some authorities believe that the name Kalāheo applies only to the upper reaches of the gulch near the town of Kalāheo and that the lower reaches were known as Kawaihaka. They have also identified the bay fronting the gulch as Lokoawa Bay.

Pālama Beach

Pele-the-great-sleeper went as far as Wahiawa and down at Lawai. She dug again and that became the fishpond of Nomilu.

Ka Loea Aina
August 26, 1899

Pālama Beach lies at the base of the most unusual fishpond in the Hawaiian Islands, Nōmilu Fishpond. Approximately 20 acres in size, the spring-fed pond is situated in Nōmilu Cone, a huge volcanic cinder hill located at the site of one of numerous vents that produced the lavas of the Kōloa Volcanic Series. The cones built at the vents range in size from small spatter cones to large cinder cones. Nōmilu Cone is composed principally of cinder that is partly cemented by calcium carbonate.

Nōmilu Fishpond, a natural salt water lake, occupies the interior floor of Nōmilu Cone. Its water level rises and falls with the tides. The pond is fed by springs, so the water is actually brackish. In the early 1900s a tunnel about 4 to 5 feet high and 4 feet wide was cut through a wall of the cone to improve the pond's circulation by connecting it with the ocean. A metal railing gate was placed in the waterway to contain the fish.

The fishpond was famous throughout Hawai'i, and in former times every chief who visited the island went to see it. The mullet raised in the pond were noted for their delicacy, but for some reason they would not breed in its waters. In former times the pond was stocked with mullet fry from a fishpond at Lāwa'i Kai, a practice that is no longer continued.

According to legend the pond was formed when Pele, goddess of the volcano, was attempting to establish a home on Kaua'i. While digging the pit, she went below sea level and struck salt water which filled the pit. In anger, she left the island in search of a new home. Local tradition, however, says that the water of Nōmilu Fishpond becomes agitated immediately before a volcanic eruption on the island of Hawai'i. Some observers have noted changes in the water's color, odor, and temperature. The yellow color, the odor of sulfur, and the increased temperature are all features commonly associated with volcanic activity. The guardians of the pond are two supernatural eels, Puhiʻula and Puhipakapaka.

Nōmilu Fishpond has been privately owned for many years by the Pālama family of Kauaʻi. They maintain the site as a family recreation area. Because of the family's long association with the fishpond, the long, straight sand beach located immediately east of Nōmilu Cone is known as Pālama Beach.

The steeply sloping beach begins at Makaokāhaʻi Point at the base of the cone and ends at the low sea cliffs that make up the shoreline to Lāwaʻi Kai. A raised shelf of rock at the water's edge lines almost the entire beach. The nearshore bottom consists of many large sections of shallow patch reefs that extend out as far as Makaokāhaʻi Point. The waves that break over these reefs are often good enough for surfing, particularly during the summer, but during periods of high surf rip currents form throughout the surf zone. When the sea is calm, swimming and snorkeling opportunities are good.

PĀLAMA. Nōmilu Fishpond is one of the most unique fishponds in Hawaiʻi. Approximately 20 acres in size, it occupies the interior floor of Nōmilu Cone, a huge volcanic cinder hill. The pond is fed by springs, but the water is brackish and rises and falls with the tides. The west end of Pālama Beach adjoins the cone at Makaokāhaʻi Point.

Lanipū'ao Rock, a small, submerged rock islet, is located directly offshore the beach. A popular scuba diving destination, it is marked by a large red buoy that is known to most divers as Pālama Buoy.

Nōmilu Fishpond and Pālama Beach are located on the shoreline of McBryde Sugar Company's cane fields. They can be reached by following the wide haul-cane road that runs from 'Ele'ele to Kōloa below Nūmila. Secondary roads border the base of Nōmilu Cone and lead to the shoreline. The beach is undeveloped. There are no facilities.

Lāwa'i Kai

Ua nani Lāwa'i e waiho nei
I ke ala kīke'e a ka manu.

Lāwa'i lies beautifully below
The winding trail of the birds.

Name Chant for Alexander McBryde

Lāwa'i is a prominent valley between the land divisions of Kalāheo and Kōloa. Lāwa'i Kai, or "seaward Lāwa'i," is the portion of the valley that borders the ocean. The entire valley was once owned by Queen Emma, the wife of Kamehameha IV. She first visited the area as a new bride in 1856. Following the death of her husband in 1870, she moved to Lāwa'i and lived there for several years. The strip of land on the cliffs to the west of Lāwa'i Kai connects the valley to Nōmilu Fishpond, which was also owned by the queen.

Lāwa'i and Nōmilu Fishpond were later purchased by Alexander McBryde. Following McBryde's death, the famous fishpond was bequeathed to the Pālama family and Lāwa'i was purchased from the McBryde Estate in 1937 by Robert Allerton, a millionaire from Chicago. Allerton, with his adopted son John Gregg Allerton, turned the lower valley into a tropical garden commonly known as the Allerton Estate. They replaced the McBryde residence with a home of their own and restored Queen Emma's cottage.

Today Lāwa'i is synonymous with the Pacific Tropical Botanical Garden. Before his death in 1964, Robert Allerton designated the upper valley for the garden site. The groundbreaking ceremony was held on January 1, 1970. When John Gregg Allerton died in 1986, the Allerton Estate also became a part of the garden.

The Pacific Tropical Botanical Garden is dedicated to tropical botany. Some of its projects include discovering new sources of medicines from tropical plants, the development of new hybrids, and the preservation of rare and endemic plants which are rapidly disappearing throughout the tropics. The 186-acre garden collects and maintains many plant varieties, including 50 types of banana and 500 species of palm. The collections are set among a series of fountains, pools, and walkways. Guided tours of the garden are conducted regularly.

The Lāwa'i Kai shoreline consists of a large bay bordered by two rocky points. The eastern point extends well into the ocean, forming the major headland of the bay. It has been planted with night-blooming cereus. The abbreviated western point marks the end of the low sea cliffs that run from Pālama Beach to Lāwa'i Kai.

A wide crescent beach lines the head of the bay between the two rocky points. The beach is fronted by a shallow sand bar that varies seasonally in width depending on the direction of the incoming surf. The shorebreak that forms on the sand bar is excellent for bodysurfing, bodyboarding, and occasionally surfing. Periods of high surf generate dangerous water conditions, particularly a pounding shorebreak and strong rip currents. Swimming and snorkeling are good during periods of calm seas.

Near the western end of the beach a high bluff stands in the backshore. It was once known as Pu'u Kiloi'a, the "fish-spotting point." In former times a spotter stationed on Pu'u Kiloi'a would direct the movements of net fishermen in the bay. From his vantage point he could easily observe the movements of fish schools coming into the bay. By signaling to the men in the canoes below, he would direct their movements in surrounding the schools of fish. *Akule,* big-eyed scad, popular pelagic schooling fish, were caught by this method and are still commonly netted here by commercial fishermen.

There is no direct public access to the beach at Lāwa'i Kai. The single access road that leads to the beach and the garden is private. However, the eastern point of the bay is accessible over an ancient Hawaiian shoreline trail that follows the low cliffs from Spouting Horn Beach Park.

Spouting Horn Beach Park

Noho i ke puhi.
Sits in the blowhole.

Jailed. One who falls into a blowhole rarely escapes.
'Ōlelo No'eau, Hawaiian Proverbs and Poetical Sayings
Pukui, 1983

Blowholes are common phenomena on rocky Hawaiian shorelines. They are usually found on flat lava benches that are directly exposed to high surf. Most blowholes are actually narrow chimneys through the roof of a sea cave or lava tube beneath the bench. During periods of high surf, breaking waves rush into the cave or lava tube, forcing a powerful blast of compressed air, spray, and whitewater up through the hole, which erupts above the bench as a spectacular salt-water fountain. Blowholes are also called spouting horns because of the unusually loud roaring noises created by the rushing air and water.

Spouting Horn Beach Park centers on the Spouting Horn, one of Hawai'i's famous blowholes. It is also one of Kaua'i's most popular tourist attractions. To accommodate the hundreds of people who visit the site daily, the park includes a paved parking area for automobiles and tour buses. There are also restrooms and a dozen curio vendor stands.

Hawaiian legend attributes the noise of this blowhole to a legendary lizard, or *mo'o,* who was caught inside the chimney. The *mo'o* was returning to Kaua'i from Ni'ihau where he had learned of the death of his two sisters. Blinded by his tears of sorrow he missed his landing nearby and got caught in the blowhole. There his voice can still be heard whenever high surf strikes the rocks.

The lava bench through which the Spouting Horn fountains is easily accessible from the lookout above it. Visitors seeking close-up pictures of the fountain should keep their distance from the actual hole in the bench, as the rocks near the hole are slippery, and unexpectedly large waves may surge across the entire bench. Over the years a number of people have lost their lives here after being swept into the blowhole or into the ocean. Only one person has ever been dragged through the Spouting Horn and lived to tell about it.

The incident occurred on August 28, 1985, and involved an 18-year-old visitor from Palo Alto, California. Chris Parr was one of five men standing 10 to 15 feet from the mouth of the blowhole when a large wave struck. The force of the whitewater knocked him down and within seconds he had been dragged into the mouth by the wave's backwash. Parr found himself at the bottom of the chimney looking 10 feet up at the opening. He quickly noted that the blowhole was L-shaped, with a horizontal tube 3 feet in diameter and half-filled with water leading out to the ocean. He knew that the next series of waves would probably crush him in the tube, so he immediately scrambled and swam his way out to the open ocean. There he treaded water until fire department personnel from Kōloa arrived and brought him ashore. Parr attributed his survival to his background in surfing and water polo.

The shoreline at Spouting Horn Beach Park is primarily rocky, generally precluding swimming. However, a small pocket of sand to the west of the lookout provides a limited swimming and sunbathing site during periods of calm seas. Commercial dive boats often bring snorkeling tours here. During periods of high surf the beach disappears, as the powerful waves that strike the shoreline quickly wash away the sand and carry it offshore. Other than the visitors who come to see the Spouting Horn, the park is visited primarily by fishermen.

A number of archaeological sites have been noted in the low sea cliffs between Lāwa'i Bay and the Spouting Horn, including a paved walking trail and several shelter caves. A colony of wedge-tailed shearwaters makes its home in this area, although the birds have suffered several losses from predation by dogs.

Kukui'ula Small Boat Harbor

Kukuiula Bay, 3 miles W of Makahuena Point, has an entrance width of 150 yards and an inland extent of 300 yards; considerable protection is afforded small craft except in S winds. There is a breakwater on the reef that extends from the SE point of the bay. Kukuiula is a settlement at the head of the bay.

National Oceanic and Atmospheric Administration, 1977

The south shore of Kaua'i from Lāwa'i to Po'ipū is considered one of the best sport diving and spearing areas on the island. These waters are especially attractive because of the normally calm seas, extensive reefs, excellent underwater visibility, and close proximity to residential and resort communities. Kukui'ula Small Boat Harbor is the only harbor along this reach; so its boat ramp, mooring areas, and boat-trailer parking lots are heavily used for both recreational and commercial activities. Other facilities at the harbor include restrooms, showers, and a large picnic pavilion in a small park.

As one of the focal points for ocean recreation on the south shore, Kukui'ula Small Boat Harbor attracts others besides boaters, including shoreline fishermen who fish from the harbor's breakwater, nearshore swimmers, and surfers on the reef outside the breakwater.

Beach House Beach
Beach House Blows Away

On the way to Spouting Horn at Po'ipu, the road abuptly stops near the figure of 'Iwa, a metal bird jutting from the peak of a frame that once defined the Beach

BEACH HOUSE. Beach House Beach, typical of the beaches in this area, is a small roadside beach that almost completely disappears at high tide. Sunbathers use the beach at low tide, but the major attractions are snorkeling in the nearshore waters and surfing on the offshore reef. The beach is named for the nearby Beach House Restaurant.

House restaurant. 'Iwa is the man-o-war bird, the name sake of the hurricane that destroyed the Beach House and the road, stores and homes that snaked along the coast to Spouting Horn.

The Garden Island
November 29, 1982

Beach House Beach lies on the leeward side of a rocky point which for many years has been the site of a restaurant. The Tahiti Longhouse, the first restaurant there, was eventually sold and renamed the Beach House. In November 1982, Hurricane 'Iwa destroyed the Beach House along with many other shoreline structures in the area. The restaurant reopened in 1984. Some long-time area residents still refer to the area as Longhouse Beach.

Beach House Beach, typical in this area, is a small, roadside beach that almost completely disappears at high tide. Sunbathers come at low tide, but the major attractions are snorkeling in the nearshore waters and surfing on the offshore reef. The reef parallels the shoreline, adjoining the point fronting the Beach House Restaurant. There, the reef is indented by a shallow embayment that is excellent for novice snorkelers.

The reef also offers three of the south shore's most popular surfing sites: P.K.s, Centers, and Acid Drops. P.K.s, short for Prince Kūhiō's, the name of a nearby park, is directly offshore of the Beach House Restaurant. It attracts surfers and bodyboarders, and many spectators who line the low sea wall fronting the restaurant to watch the action offshore. Centers, the second of the three breaks, is located in the center of the little bay. It is primarily a surfing break. The third site, Acid Drops, is located at the western end of the bay and breaks the farthest offshore. Its steep waves form on a shallow patch reef, creating a very exciting drop or take-off when a surfer first catches a wave. The name Acid Drops is a play on words that originated in the 1960s. It refers to the steep drop in the waves and to the fact that a number of surfers at that time were "dropping acid," that is, experimenting with the illegal drug commonly called acid.

Public restrooms, showers, and a paved parking area are located directly across the road from Beach House Beach.

Prince Kūhiō Park

In Memory of
Ke Alii A Na Makaainana
(The Chief of the People)
Jonah Kuhio Kalanianaole
Delegate to Congress
1902–1922
March 26, 1871   January 7, 1922
Makua Aina Hoopulapula
(Father [of the] Homestead Lands)
Plaque inscription
Prince Kūhiō Park

Prince Kūhiō Park is located on the shoreline of Ho'ai Bay. The park is a historical site that commemorates the birthplace of Prince Jonah Kūhiō Kalaniana'ole. Prince Kūhiō, the son of Kekaulike Kinoiki II and High Chief David Kahalepouli Pi'ikoi, was born on March 26, 1871, here at Ho'ai. His mother died soon after his birth. He and his two older brothers were adopted by his mother's sister, Kapi'olani, and her husband Kalākaua, who had no children of their own. When Kalākaua ascended the throne in 1874 as king of the Hawaiian Islands, he gave each of the boys the title of prince.

Kalākaua was succeeded by his sister, Lili'uokalani. In the revolution of 1893 the monarchy was overthrown. Prince Kūhiō, with other Royalists loyal to the deposed queen, was involved in an unsuccessful attempt to overthrow the Republic of Hawai'i that had replaced the monarchy. He served one year as a political prisoner and was released on October 8, 1896.

In 1902 Prince Kūhiō was elected Hawai'i's second delegate to Congress. Hawai'i had become a territory of the United States in 1898 and as such was allowed one non-voting delegate. He served from November 1902 until his death in January 1922. Prince Kūhiō is probably best remembered for his successful efforts in behalf of the Hawaiian Homes Commission Act, by which certain public lands were to be made available to native Hawaiians for homesteads. Homestead lands today are found on five of the eight major Hawaiian islands largely as a result of his efforts.

Although Prince Kūhiō Park is located on the shoreline, it is maintained as a passive park for strollers and sightseers rather than as a beach park for beachgoers.

Facilities include restrooms and parking. Several small pockets of sand are located along the margins of Hoʻai Bay across the road from the park, and a large, secluded pocket of sand known as Waterhouse Beach is located between Hoʻai Bay and Kōloa Landing. The sand at these beaches almost completely disappears at high tide, but provides swimming, snorkeling, and sunbathing sites when the ocean recedes at low tide.

Kōloa Landing

The village of Koloa is fifteen miles to the northeast of Waimea, and ten miles south from Lihue. It has no harbor, but an open roadstead. The trade wind blows along and a little off shore. The anchorage is close in shore, in four or six fathoms, under the shelter of a bluff. The town is two miles from the landing, and is noted for its sugar plantation.

Hawaiian Guide Book
Whitney, 1875

The town of Kōloa, gateway to the Poʻipū resort area, was established in 1835 by three Americans. Peter Brinsmade, William Hooper, and William Ladd, the principals of Ladd and Company, leased a large tract of land at Kōloa where for several years they ran a sugar plantation and a mill. Historians acknowledge this venture as the first successful commercial sugar plantation in the Hawaiian Islands. Ladd and Company was dissolved in 1845, but Kōloa Plantation and the town that developed with it remained and continued to grow.

Prior to the introduction of motorized vehicles and roads, ships provided the major means of transportion for Hawaiʻi's plantations, so every plantation had its own landing. Kōloa Landing was established in Hanakaʻape Bay in a natural cove cut into the shoreline by Waikomo Stream. Before the turn of the century, an average of 40 to 60 ships, including whalers, called each year at the landing. There they discharged and picked up cargo and passengers and took on supplies. With the introduction of modern means of transportation, the old sugar landings fell into disuse. Kōloa Landing was used into the 1920s, but today little more than its name remains to identify this once busy site.

Kōloa Landing is located at the western end of Hoʻonani Road. It's rocky shoreline attracts fishermen, while its nearshore waters are much used by snorkelers

and scuba divers. The landing is a popular site for patrons of commercial diving tours who enjoy exploring the bottom features, including tunnels and caves, and watching the wide variety of fish. Water conditions are excellent throughout the year except during periods of high surf and *kona*, or southerly, storms.

Poʻipū Beach

Construction of the Sheraton-Kauai Hotel began yesterday on approximately 10 acres of Knudson Trust land at Poipu Beach when Leonard L. Gorrel of the Hawaii Sheraton Corp. broke ground with a replica of an ancient oʻo digging stick.

Situated on a white sand beach 500 yards long, the 150 room hotel will be built by Haas and Haynie Corp. at a cost of $3.5 million.

Honolulu Advertiser
April 14, 1967

Poʻipū is the south shore's most popular tourist destination. The Sheraton Kauaʻi Resort, one of the major resorts in the Poʻipū area, is situated on Poʻipū Beach, a pocket beach that lies in a small bay between two rocky points. The beach is very heavily used by sunbathers, snorkelers, swimmers, bodysurfers, bodyboarders, surfers, and windsurfers. On a typical sunny day when the surf is up and the trade winds are blowing, parking near the single public right-of-way is always at a premium.

Poʻipū Beach is a popular windsurfing site. Trade winds occasionally make for excellent sailing, and the beach is close to the road, an important consideration for windsurfers with their cumbersome gear. A series of reefs offshore of the hotel provide a good range of conditions for bodyboarders and surfers of varying abilities. Beginners find small, gentle waves near the beach, surfers of intermediate ability ride a slightly larger break approximately 100 yards offshore, and during periods of high surf, experts surf First Break, an open ocean break nearly half a mile out. Dangerous water conditions occur during periods of high surf, particularly a heavy shorebreak, strong backwash, and powerful rip currents.

The public right-of-way to the beach is found at the eastern end of Hoʻonani Road. Except for a shower, there are no public facilities. At the western end of the

Po'ɪpū. The Sheraton Kaua'i Resort was built on Po'ipū Beach in the late 1960s. A public right-of-way at the end of Ho'onani Road leads through the resort to the beach. It is well used by a wide variety of ocean recreation enthusiasts including surfers, windsurfers, bodyboarders, swimmers, snorkelers, and sunbathers.

Sheraton Kaua'i Resort at the intersection of Ho'onani Road and Kapili Road, another public right-of-way with a small landscaped parking lot is located on a low rocky point. Although there is no sand beach here, the surf that forms on the shallow reef fronting the point is regarded as one of the best bodysurfing and bodyboarding breaks on the south shore. The site is known as Cowshead.

Wai'ōhai Beach

Kihahouna *heiau,* even in its highly altered state, is still very much part of Kaua'i County's inventory of cultural resources. The local population, especially the Hawaiian community, still feel a psychological attachment to the site, and I am confident in saying that this is the general feeling among other ethinic groups as well.

Here is a prehistoric Hawaiian site that will be saved, preserved and maintained without any State or County aid, without any money from ethnic organizations. It will be financed entirely by AmFac, Inc. and Waiohai Resort. This is most extraordinary.

> "Assessment of Damage to Historical and Archaeological Resources Resulting from Hurricane 'Iwa"
> Kikuchi, 1983

The first Western-style building on Wai'ōhai Beach was a simple wooden shack. It was built by Anne Sinclair Knudsen, wife of Valdemar Knudsen, one of Hawai'i's first sugar planters. Knudsen arrived on Kaua'i in 1854 at the age of 33. He was founder of Kekaha Sugar Company and also purchased large tracts of land in the

69

Kōloa and Poʻipū areas, including the beach at Waiʻō-hai. In 1868, Knudsen married Anne Sinclair, one of the daughters of Elizabeth Sinclair, the Scottish matriarch who purchased Niʻihau in 1864. Anne Sinclair Knudsen decided that the family should have a beach home in Poʻipū, and she selected the beach at Waiʻōhai.

The shack was followed by a permanent house, large enough to accommodate visitors. It included a separate dining hall and cookhouse. In later years Knudsen's son Eric moved the beach house and connected it to the dining hall and cookhouse to create a single large home. The Knudsen home was a landmark on the site until 1962 when it was demolished to make way for the original Waiʻōhai Hotel.

The Waiʻōhai Hotel, the first hotel in Poʻipū, was a 50-room low rise built among the trees. Famous for its hospitality and its Sunday brunches on an open terrace facing the ocean, it led the way for the development of Poʻipū as a major visitor industry resort destination. In 1979 it was demolished and replaced by a much larger complex, the Stouffer Waiʻōhai Beach Resort. However, the Sunday brunch still continues as part of the Waiʻō-hai tradition.

Waiʻōhai Beach is a narrow sand crescent that lines a small bay. Situated in the lee of Nukumoi Point, it offers good swimming and excellent snorkeling opportunities. A sand channel runs into the center of the beach. Offshore, at the edge of the reef, is a popular surfing site known as Waiʻōhai. High surf generates good surfing waves, but also brings dangerous near-shore conditions, particularly strong rip currents that flow in a westerly direction.

Public facilities are located in adjoining Poʻipū Beach Park.

Poʻipū Beach Park. Poʻipū Beach Park, the south shore's most popular beach park, is heavily used by residents and visitors, especially on weekends and holidays. One of the park's main attractions is its sheltered swimming area, which is suitable for families with young children. At low tide the sand on Nukumoi Point is exposed and attracts sunbathers and strollers.

Po‘ipū Beach Park

Except for a few shortcomings, Poipu is developing as it was scheduled to develop, said Kauai Planning Department Director Brian Nishimoto, who was in on the development of the plans a decade ago. Some people protest change, but the county has designated Poipu as a resort area and thus ensured change.

What has shocked many people is the speed with which the development has occurred in recent years, after a lull during the majority of the 1970s.

Sunday Star-Bulletin & Advertiser
May 18, 1980

Po‘ipū Beach Park, the south shore's most popular beach park, is much used by residents and visitors, particularly on weekends and holidays. One of the main attractions of this large park is its safe swimming beach. Although the beach is but a small pocket of sand, its shallow nearshore waters are protected by a short breakwater to the east and by Nukumoi Point to the west, creating a sheltered nearshore swimming area. Small waves forming on the shallow sand bar immediately offshore of the beach attract many bodyboarders. During periods of high surf, a rip current flows through the surfing site. Warning signs are posted onshore.

At the western edge of the park is an interesting example of a geological shoreline feature called a tombolo. Tombolos are sand bars that build across the ocean bottom from one island to another, or from shore to an island. Just such a sand bar, built between the shoreline of the park and a shallow rock islet offshore made Nukumoi Point. In all of the eight major Hawaiian islands, there are only three tombolos, and all of them are on Kaua‘i. The second is located at Crater Hill on the north shore, where a sand bar joins the base of the hill to Makapili Island, and the third is located at Kīpū Kai where a sand bar joins Mōlehu Point to Kīpū Kai Beach. Nukumoi Point is a popular site for pole and throw-net fishing and occasionally for skimboarding.

Facilities in Po‘ipū Beach Park include restrooms, showers, a lifeguard tower, and a parking area. The park is located at Ho‘owili and Po‘ipū Beach roads.

Brennecke Beach

The County Council is studying a joint proposal with a citizens group to buy a parcel of land near Brennecke Beach in Poipu to preserve the beach, one of the top bodysurfing spots in Hawaii.

The beach, which is a popular tourist attraction, was ravaged by Hurricane ‘Iwa in November 1982. Much of the sand was swept out to sea.

Brennecke, a former plantation doctor, has decided not to rebuild a house on the lot destroyed during the hurricane.

Honolulu Star-Bulletin
November 16, 1984

Brennecke Beach in Po‘ipū is one of the most popular bodysurfing and bodyboarding beaches on Kaua‘i. The beach itself is little more than a pocket of sand at the edge of Ho‘owili Road, but a shallow nearshore sand bar is responsible for the site's real attraction, its shorebreak waves. The waves are usually best during the summer months when high surf on the south shore is common. High surf generates the powerful shorebreak that attracts wave riding enthusiasts. It also causes strong rip currents. County lifeguards and fire department personnel make many rescues here every year.

The sand bar at Brennecke is small and often congested with swimmers, bodysurfers, and bodyboarders. For this reason, a 1972 state regulation prohibits surfboards in the nearshore waters, which would be a real hazard to everyone else in the water. The off-limits area is defined by an imaginary line from the point offshore Po‘ipū Beach Park to the point at Ma‘a Road.

Brennecke Beach was named for Dr. Marvin Brennecke who for many years owned a home on a sea wall adjoining the beach. Brennecke came to Kaua‘i in 1931 as the assistant plantation doctor at Līhu‘e Plantation. He continued working as a plantation doctor for the rest of his career, and spent his final 30 years, from 1942 until his retirement in 1972, employed by Waimea and Kekaha plantations, Gay and Robinson Sugar Company, and Olokele Sugar Company.

In 1934 Brennecke bought a beachfront lot in Po‘ipū from Antone Vindinha, later to be mayor of Kaua‘i. Brennecke build a beach house on the lot several years later, a modest dwelling which he remodeled and expanded in December 1941.

On November 23, 1982, the Brennecke home, by that time a landmark, was destroyed by Hurricane ‘Iwa, when it was swept off its foundation slab and pushed across Poʻipū Beach Road. The hurricane's massive waves thoroughly scoured Brennecke Beach and left only large boulders in place of the vanished sand. The road behind the beach was undermined and washed out to sea.

Although it took several years for the beach to recover, the sand eventually returned to Brennecke Beach and covered many of the boulders that were exposed or pushed inshore. The beach has regained its original size and is still a very popular bodysurfing and bodyboarding site.

Shipwreck Beach

Keoniloa Beach at Koloa, Kauai, Hawaiian Islands, on which the "pictured rocks" are found, lies between the sand-stone cliffs of Makawahi on the east and the lava cliffs of Makahuena on the west. The beach is about one half a mile in length; at the western end near the pictured sand stone ledge is the small boat landing of Kaneaukai.

Thrum's Hawaiian Annual
1898

The shipwreck that gives the beach its name was an unidentified wooden boat that lay on the sand at the water's edge for many years. It was battered by storms and stripped by people hunting firewood, but its ribs and keel survived the assaults. Then on November 23, 1982, Hurricane ʻIwa devastated the south shore of Kauaʻi and destroyed what little remained of the shipwreck. Today only its heavy, rusted motor remains, buried in the sand, where it is occasionally exposed during periods of high surf.

Keoneloa, the Hawaiian name of the beach, meaning

SHIPWRECK BEACH. Makawehi Point, a high bluff of lithified sand dunes, is the most prominent landmark at Shipwreck Beach. The shipwreck of Shipwreck Beach lay for many years in the lee of the point in front of the sunbather. Today only the heavily rusted motor of the wreck remains, buried in the sand, where it is occasionally exposed during periods of high surf.

"the long sands," is a historic site noted for its petro-glyphs. Petroglyphs are usually associated with lava fields near ancient trails, but the Hawaiians also carved them into the soft beachrock shelves here, and also far-ther down the coast at Maha'ulepu. Only extremely severe southwesterly winter storms expose these unique art forms. These storms seem to scour the beaches much more drastically than do others, stripping away more sand to uncover the beachrock shelves below.

Today, Shipwreck Beach is best known as a bodysurf-ing, bodyboarding, and windsurfing site. The bodysurf-ing and bodyboarding take place nearshore at the east-ern end of the beach where a low rocky bench that fronts most of the shoreline opens onto an unobstructed sand beach in the lee of Makawehi Point. High surf periodically generates a pounding shorebreak and pow-erful rip currents, but it also brings some of the best bodysurfing and bodyboarding on the island. Contests for both sports have been held here periodically since 1982.

Shipwreck Beach is an important windsurfing site. Windsurfers launch at the eastern end of the beach to sail offshore and wave-jump in the surf outside the point. Surfers also ride the various breaks in this area; and Makawehi Point, a high, white, lithified sand dune bluff, provides good opportunities for pole fishermen.

Shipwreck Beach is reached by following Po'ipū Road to its eastern end. There the pavement ends and a wide cane-haul road continues. A dirt road turns off to the beach from the cane-haul road near the end of the paved road and leads to an unpaved parking area inland of Makawehi Point. There are no public facilities.

Māhā'ulepū Beach

Mt. Ha'upu towers over the ahupua'a of Maha'ulepu from Pu'u Pihakapu in the east to Ka lae o Kahonu in the west.

Along the shore, lithified calcareous sand dunes extend below sea level, and were formed when the sea stood about 60 feet lower than now. Moderately to well cemented calcareous sand dunes are found along the coast from Makahu'ena Point eastward. It appears that the cementation of the first inch or so of the surface lay-ers has taken place by the solution of calcium carbonate at the surface, and its rapid deposition almost immedi-ately below the surface.

"The Archaeology of Kona, Kaua'i, Nā Ahupua'a Weliweli, Pa'a, Māhā'ulepū"
Ching, Palama, and Stauder, 1974

Māhā'ulepū Beach is a 2-mile reach of coast that winds from Punahoa Point to Hā'ula Beach. It includes some of the most beautiful shoreline on Kaua'i's south shore. This area is of great scientific importance, to archaeolo-gists, biologists, and geologists. It is also an important ocean recreation area, being close to the island's centers of population and having excellent recreational re-sources.

Historians have reported that many pre-contact ar-chaeological sites were probably destroyed when the Māhā'ulepū lands were cleared for sugar cane cultiva-tion, but they believe that the remaining sites indicate that the area was once well populated. The British explorer Captain George Vancouver noted in the 1790s that the coastal plain was brightly lit with campfires, and the numerous sand dune burial sites seem to con-firm that Māhā'ulepū was once well settled with Hawai-ians. The fertile inland valley and the productive near-shore fishing grounds would have combined to make an ideal area for habitation.

Points of geologic interest at Māhā'ulepū vary widely in age and degree of weathering. Both the older Waimea Canyon Volcanic Series and the younger Kōloa Volcanic Series are represented, the former by Hā'upu, the deeply eroded remnant of a caldera on the flank of the main Kaua'i shield volcano, and the latter by a cluster of cinder and spatter cones. The cones mark a small concentration of the 40 vents that have been identified as the primary eruption sites of the Kōloa Volcanic Series. The Māhā'ulepū shoreline also contains a num-ber of littoral features that show some of the results of interaction between land and water. These include lithi-fied sand dunes; limestone hills, sinks, and caves, which are the eroded remnants of raised coral reefs; wave-cut terraces, nips, sea cliffs, and a small sea stack.

The Māhā'ulepū shoreline is very rich in other re-sources. In the sand dunes are fossil remains of extinct birds, including three species of goose, a long-legged owl, and a flightless rail. Flocks of seabirds still gravitate to the beaches and water birds to several natural ponds and man-made siltation basins. A colony of wedge-tailed shearwaters nests on one of the cliff faces. The sand dunes support a variety of native strand vegetation such as *naupaka, 'ilima, pōhu'ehu'e,* and *pa'u o Hi'iaka,* in addition to introduced vegetation such as ironwood trees and *koa haole.* Several caves in the vicinity contain two extremely rare insects, one a blind wolf spider and the other a blind terrestrial amphipod. In its natural and historical resources, Māhā'ulepū is unique.

The beach is a very important ocean recreation area. Activities include beachcombing, picnicking, sunbathing, swimming, pole fishing, spear fishing, seaweed gathering, snorkeling, scuba diving, surfing, bodysurfing, bodyboarding, kayaking, and windsurfing. Beachgoers generally recognize three distinct areas at Māhā'ulepū: Gillin's Beach, Kawailoa Bay, and Hā'ula Beach.

Gillin's Beach was named for Elbert Gillin, a longtime supervisor for Grove Farm Company, the owner of the Māhā'ulepū plantation lands. Gillin arrived in Hawai'i in 1912. For a number of years he worked on Maui where he helped engineer the large bridge over 'Ohe'o Stream in Kīpahulu. In 1925 he moved to Kaua'i

MĀHĀ'ULEPŪ. Māhā'ulepū Beach is a two-mile reach of coast that winds from Punahoa Point to Hā'ula Beach and includes Gillin's Beach and Kawailoa Bay, pictured here. As the last major undeveloped beach in proximity to the island's centers of population, it is an important ocean recreation area. Māhā'ulepū Beach is also one of Kaua'i's most scenic shoreline areas, offering many interesting coastal features including raised coral reefs, sea cliffs, and a sea stack.

where he is remembered as the construction superintendent of the Hāʻupu Range Tunnel. The half-mile-long tunnel through the range provides cane-haul trucks with direct access from the fields on the north side of the mountain range to the Kōloa mill on the south side. During his employment with Grove Farm, Gillin built a beach home at Māhāʻulepū, the only structure on the entire beach.

Gillin's Beach lies between Punahoa and Kamala points. It is a long, narrow sand crescent that is backed by vegetated sand dunes. Broken patches of beachrock line most of the beach. The Gillin beach home, a single-story white house in a coconut grove, sits in the backshore midway along the beach.

On January 7, 1980, a severe winter storm struck the south shore and began eroding the beach fronting the Gillin home. By January 9, the high surf had claimed over 6 feet of sand beach. The severe erosion uncovered three large shelves of beachrock, each containing numerous petroglyphs. Beachcombers watching the storm activity found the historic figures, and from them news of this previously unrecorded petroglyph field spread quickly. Among the first visitors were several native Hawaiians who claimed that they were guided to the site by a rainbow. This incident gave the site its name, the Rainbow Petroglyphs.

Petroglyphs are often found in areas where Hawaiians rested or camped during journeys on foot or by canoe. It is not uncommon to find designs showing modern influence mixed in with the ancient designs, indicating that the same rest stops were still being used after the discovery of Hawaiʻi by non-Hawaiians. Prominent figures among the Rainbow Petroglyphs were humans, animals, crab's-claw-shaped canoe sails, and some more modern designs, including a star and some letters and names. When the storm that exposed the Rainbow Petroglyphs abated after several days, the ocean immediately began restoring sand to the denuded beach. Within two weeks all of the petroglyphs had been completely covered again.

Kawailoa Bay, the most popular shoreline area at Māhāʻulepū, is an exceptionally beautiful south-shore site located between Kamala and Pāʻoʻo points. Kamala Point, the western end of the bay, is covered with low sand dunes vegetated primarily by *naupaka* and ironwoods. The beach that winds around the point, the widest beach at Māhāʻulepū, includes several shallow sand-bottomed pockets for swimmers. The largest of these pockets is found seaward of the point, where a broken semicircle of rocks offshore offers some protection to the nearshore waters. Many of the beachrock shelves at the water's edge along the point are covered with *limu ʻeleʻele,* a popular edible seaweed.

From the center of Kawailoa Bay where the sand beach ends, to Pāʻoʻo Point, the eastern point of the bay, the shoreline consists of a low limestone sea cliff covered with active and lithified sand dunes. These vegetated dunes are covered primarily with grass, backed by stands of ironwoods. The sea cliffs below the dunes have been deeply undercut by high surf and are indented by inlets and caves. The landmark feature in the area is a small mushroom-shaped sea stack that projects above a shallow reef next to the outer point. The point and the reef adjoining it offer some protection to the inner bay during normal trade wind conditions.

Hāʻula Beach is the last beach along the Māhāʻulepū shoreline. It is a pocket beach located at the head of a large cove between Pāʻoʻo and Nāʻakea points. Unlike the beaches at Gillins and Kawailoa Bay, it cannot be reached by road. Beachgoers park on the east side of Pāʻoʻo Point and follow a trail over the low sea cliffs to the shore.

The small straight beach lies at the base of the ʻĀweoweo sand dunes, the highest sand dunes on the south shore. At over 100 feet in elevation, they rival the height of the famous dunes of the Barking Sands in Mānā. A low, flat, rock shelf fronts the entire beach, except for a narrow sand channel in its center. The marginal swimming conditions and its isolation leave Hāʻula Beach deserted much of the time except for fishermen and nudists. During periods of high seas, waves inundate the entire beach and wash up on the dunes. This is indicated by the high vegetation line on the face of the dunes. The rocky points on either side of the beach support a variety of native coastal plants including *ʻilima, paʻu o Hiʻiaka, naupaka,* and *pua pilo.*

The Māhāʻulepū shoreline is the last significant undeveloped shoreline near the population centers of the island. For this reason it has for many years been an important recreational area for local residents. Most of the land bordering the Māhāʻulepū shoreline is owned by the Grove Farm Company and leased by the McBryde Sugar Company. The only automobile access to the area is over the plantation's cane-haul roads. The sugar company allows public access over its roads to the beach, but reserves the right to terminate it at any time.

To reach Māhāʻulepū from Kōloa, take Kōloa Road to Weliweli Road. Pass San Raphael Church and go 3 miles past Kōloa Mill. Māhāʻulepū is also accessible from the cane-haul road that leads to Shipwreck Beach. There are no facilities anywhere at Māhāʻulepū.

Kīpū Kai

No Kīpū Kai ke aloha	For Kīpū Kai is my affection
Home i ka pili kahakai	Where there's a home beside the sea
I laila au i ʻike ai	It was there that I found
I ka nui loko maikaʻi.	Such unbounded hospitality.
Nanea i ka hoʻolohe	I enjoy listening quietly
Ka halulu mai o ke kai	To the roar of the sea
Ka nalu nui e holu ana	As large waves come rolling in
I ka lae a o Kuahonu.	To Kuahonu Point.
Pau ʻole koʻu hoʻohihi	Endless is my admiration
I ka nani a o Hāʻupu	For the beauty of Hāʻupu
Mauna kiʻekiʻe i luna	A hill, so high above
Hanohano ke ʻike aku.	Majestic to my sight.
Makemake wale ka ikena	It is delightful to see
I nā manu pikake nani	The pretty peacocks
E kakaʻi a haʻheo ana	Strutting by together
I ka malu a o ke kiawe.	In the shade of the kiawe trees.
Puana ʻia me ke aloha	Thus ends my song with affection
No ka nani a o Hāʻupu	For the beauty of Hāʻupu
Me Keaka lokomaikaʻi	And for Jack, the kind hearted
Ka haku a o Kīpū Kai.	The owner of Kīpū Kai.

"Kīpū Kai"
Song by Mary Kawena Pukuʻi

The Hāʻupu Range is a massive mountain that stands alone on the southeast flank of the Kauaʻi shield volcano. It is made up of thick, hard lava flows that once accumulated in a large pit crater. Erosion has removed the less-resistant lavas that once surrounded it, leaving the crater fill, now the mountain range, standing in magnificent isolation on the shoreline of the island.

Kīpū Kai is a unique coastal valley located on the seaward side of the Hāʻupu Range. It lies between Māhāʻulepū and Nāwiliwili, isolated from the rest of the island by high mountain ridges. The valley contains much of archaeological interest, including springs, house sites, temple sites, and petroglyphs. Kamapuaʻa, the *kupua*, or demi-god, who could assume the shape of a pig or a man, is associated in legendary accounts with a number of the archaeological sites. One of these is Waiakapuaʻa, "water [used] by the pig [Kamapuaʻa]," a spring where he once slept.

Kīpū Kai has been privately owned and operated as a cattle ranch for many years. The last owner of the 1,096-acre ranch was John T. Waterhouse who died on February 20, 1984. In 1977 Waterhouse made an extremely generous gift to the state of Hawaiʻi, deeding the entire ranch to the state, but stipulating that the state's ownership is to take effect only following the

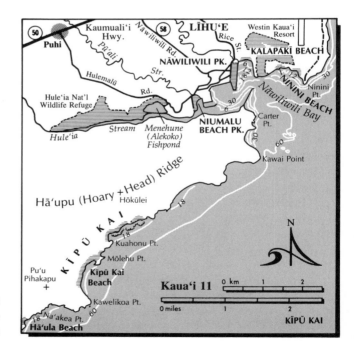

lifetimes of his nieces, Cherry Ann Waterhouse Suther-land, Dicksie Lee Waterhouse Sandifer, Barbara Hurd Tosschi, Sue Anna Waterhouse Wells, and nephew Sandy Waterhouse. The lands of Kīpū Kai will eventually revert to the state, but probably not until midway through the twenty-first century.

In making his gift, Waterhouse expressed the hope that Kīpū Kai would be used "as a nature, animal, and wildlife preserve" and hoped it would provide a "meaningful educational experience" for the people of Hawai'i. In keeping with these ideas Waterhouse himself introduced a small flock of *nēnē* to Kīpū Kai. The *nēnē* is an endangered native Hawaiian goose, the offi-cial state bird. *Nēnē* are found in limited numbers on the islands of Hawai'i and Maui, but had died out on Kaua'i. Waterhouse aquired his *nēnē* from Herbert Shipman of Kea'au on Hawai'i whose birds were part of the breeding stock for the state's captive rearing project. The *nēnē* at Kīpū Kai fared well and were eventually freed to roam the ranch lands in the mid-1980s. They began ranging outside Kīpū Kai and appear to have suc-cessfully reestablished themselves in the wild. They have been spotted as close as Māhā'ulepū and as far away as Ahukini.

The Kīpū Kai shoreline is an important recreational area. It is 2 miles long and consists of a series of four

KĪPŪ KAI. High surf rolls into the longest beach on the Kīpū Kai shoreline. During periods of calm seas tour boats from Nā-wiliwili Harbor come here to snorkel and picnic. They anchor inside the shelter of the cove formed by the intersection of the beach and Mōlehu Point. Kīpū Kai Valley to the rear of the beach is privately owned, so there is no public access to the area by land.

beaches divided by low points of rock. The first and longest of the beaches is located between Kawelikoa and Mōlehu points. Commonly known as Kīpū Kai Beach, it is a good place for a wide variety of ocean recreation activities including swimming, snorkeling, bodysurfing, bodyboarding, surfing, fishing, and beachcombing. The southwestern end of the beach is a beachcomber's paradise. The tradewinds and the prevailing currents sweep into this corner and deposit bottles, fishing floats, driftwood, and other debris. From this area to the beachrock in its center, the beach is fronted by a shallow sand bar. The shorebreak on the sand bar produces waves suitable for surfing, bodysurfing, and bodyboarding. At the northeastern end of the beach, Mōlehu Point curves into the ocean to form a protected cove and anchorage. It is a popular snorkeling destination for tour boats, particularly during the winter months when high surf precludes tours along the Nā Pali coast. Mōlehu Point is formed of lithified sand dunes and is also an example of a tombolo, an emergent sand bar which joins an islet to the mainland. Ironwoods line the low, vegetated sand dunes in the backshore.

The second beach at Kīpū Kai is located on the eastern side of Mōlehu Point. A small storm beach, bordered at the water's edge by beachrock, it offers good opportunities for fishing.

Kīpū Kai's third beach is located inshore of Kuahonu Point. It is a sand crescent that borders a small bay. A beachrock shelf lines almost the entire beach at the water's edge except for a small open pocket where the sand meets the point. Swimming conditions are marginal over the shallow, rocky bottom, but fishing opportunities are good. The Kīpū Kai ranch house is located on a grassy knoll immediately inland of the beach.

The last beach at Kīpū Kai is located below Hokulei peak. It is a narrow storm beach that consists of coral rubble and several pockets of sand. A shallow rocky shelf fronts the entire beach. It is a good place for beachcombing.

Kīpū Kai is not accessible to the public by land. The single road that leads over the high ridges of the Hā'upu Range is private property and blocked by gates. Most visitors to the area come by boat, a few by kayak. By mutual agreement between the tour boat companies and the Waterhouse Estate, the tour operations are confined to Kīpū Kai Beach, the best of the four beaches.

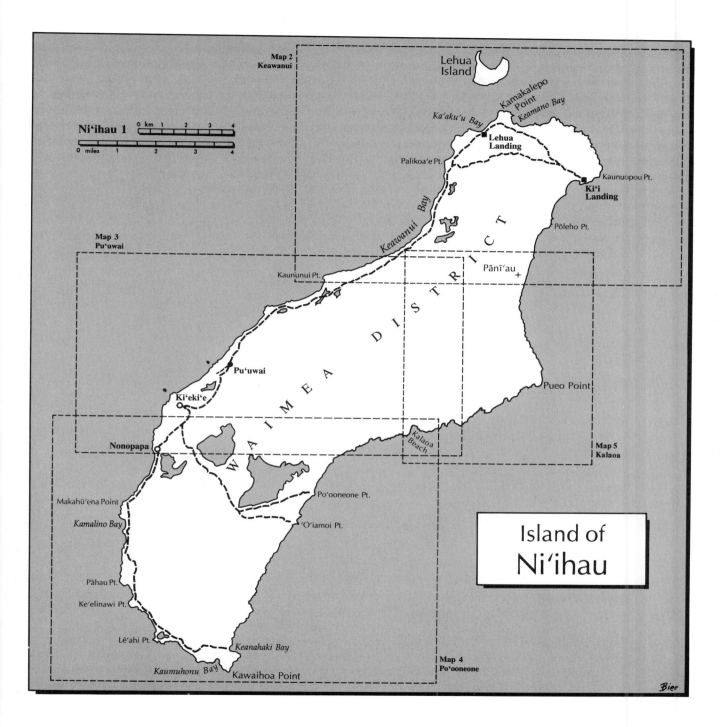

Ni'ihau 1

0 km 1 2 3 4
0 miles 1 2 3 4

Map 2
Keawanui

Lehua
Island

Kamakalepo
Point

Ka'aku'u Bay
Keamano Bay

Lehua
Landing

Palikoa'e Pt.

Kaunuopou Pt.

Ki'i
Landing

Pōleho Pt.

Map 3
Pu'uwai

Keawanui Bay

Kaununui Pt.

Pānī'au +

W A I M E A   D I S T R I C T

Pu'uwai

Pueo Point

Ki'eki'e

Nonopapa

Kalaoa
Beach

Map 5
Kalaoa

Makahū'ena Point

Po'ooneone Pt.

Kamalino Bay

'O'iamoi Pt.

Island of
Ni'ihau

Pāhau Pt.

Ke'elinawi Pt.

Lē'ahi Pt.

Keanahaki Bay

Kaumuhonu Bay
Kawaihoa Point

Map 4
Po'ooneone

Bier

Keamano Beach

E ke Au Okoa: Aloha oe.

Eia malalo nei na inoa o na makani o Niihau, ka Moku-puni o ka haole, e hoike no au i ka hana a kela a me keia makani, e hoomaka ana kona helu ana ma ka Akau.

O Ka Naulu. He makani malie maikai, aia no keia makani ma ke alo mai o Niihau, o ka waiwai hoi a keia makani he hiki ia ia ke lawe aku i ka waa e holo ana mai Niihau aku a Waimea, Kauai, me ke anuanu nui ole, ua like keia makani me ka Eka o Kona ma Hawaii, o ka Makalii ka wa hiki nui mai a keia makani.

To *Ke Au Okoa:* Greetings.

Here are the names of the winds of Ni'ihau, the haole island. I will describe the action of each wind as listed, beginning at the north.

The Naulu. This is a pleasant, calm wind. This wind is in the path of Niihau. The value of this wind is that it can take a canoe from Niihau to Waimea, Kauai without extreme coldness. It is similar to the Eka wind of Kona, Hawaii. This wind comes during the season of Makalii.

Ke Au Okoa
July 24, 1865

The shoreline on the northern tip of the island is mostly rocky except for several storm beaches and two small crescents of sand to the east of Kīkepa Point. The largest expanse of sandy shoreline along this reach is Keamano Beach, located between Kīkepa and Kamakalepo points at the head of Keamano Bay. This beautiful crescent of sand is 0.75 mile long and an average of 75 feet wide. It is narrow at its eastern end, but widens con-

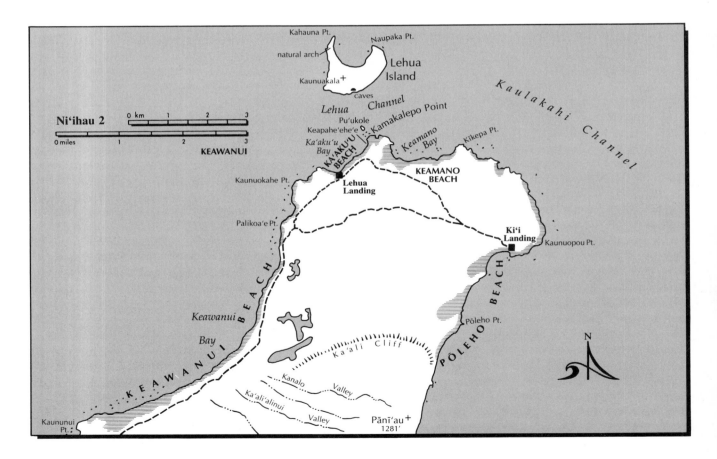

KEAMANO. Keamano Bay in the foreground is the northernmost of Ni'ihau's major beaches. It is separated from Ka'aku'u Bay (in the distance) by Kamakalepo Point, one of the landing sites of the Ni'ihau tour helicopters. The helicopters also land at the southern end of the island near Keanahaki Bay.

siderably as it curves westward. Low sand dunes on the backshore slope gently inland for several hundreds of yards to a cattle pen. The dunes are blanketed by grass and 'ilima. At the western end of the bay, the beach is completely exposed to the open ocean. The prevailing winds and currents sweep into this recessed corner and deposit masses of driftwood, fishing floats, bottles, and other debris onshore.

The bottom drops quickly to overhead depths near the shore. Strong currents occur at all times of the year. High surf generates dangerous water conditions, particularly a pounding shorebreak, a strong backwash, and powerful rip currents. During the winter, high surf inundates Keamano Bay and all of the shoreline from the northern end of the island to Kaunuopou Point.

A large, shallow sand-bottomed pool is located among the rocks on the western point of the bay. During the summer, the semicircle of lava rock that surrounds the pool protects it from the open ocean.

Kamakalepo Point, the western point of Keamano Bay, is one of the two landing sites on the island for Ni'ihau Helicopters Inc., an air tour service, started in June 1987, that is owned and operated by Ni'ihau Ranch. The tours originate on Kaua'i, make two brief stops on Ni'ihau, and then return to Kaua'i. The second tour landing site is at Keanahaki near the southern tip of the island. The helicopter is also used to transport family members and employees between Kaua'i and Ni'ihau and to take Ni'ihau residents to Kaua'i in medical emergencies.

Ka'aku'u Beach

O Ka Lehua. Aia no keia makani makai pono o ka Mokupuni o Lehua, ua ane like no kona pa ana me ka Naulu, hoeueu iki mai nae hoi keia makani, kele lua keia makani mai Niihau aku Waimea, he makani paina poi no makou ma Niihau, no ka poi ole, hookahi no pai poi, lawa na hale elima o kahi hookahi.

81

LEHUA. Lehua Island lies three-quarters of a mile offshore the northern tip of Niʻihau. Like Kawaihoa Point, the southern tip of Niʻihau, Lehua Island is a tuff cone containing blocks of basalt and limestone. Steep sea cliffs comprise the island's southern face seen here, while the opposite side of the island is an open, crescent-shaped bay.

The Lehua. This wind is located directly makai of the island of Lehua. It blows like the Naulu; however, this wind stirs a bit and carries dampness from Niihau to Waimea. This is our poi-eating wind on Niihau. When there is no poi, a single blowing of this wind is sufficient for five homes situated in one place.

[This is a play on words, a *kaona. Lehua* also refers to the Lehua variety of taro which is made into poi. Taro is not grown on Niʻihau, but the wind represents the poi which is brought to Niʻihau in sufficient quantity to satisfy the residents there.]

Ke Au Okoa
July 24, 1865

Kaʻakuʻu Beach is the first of four long beaches that wrap around the northwestern coast of Niʻihau. These four—Kaʻakuʻu, Keawanui, Kauwaha, and Puʻuwai—span the 10 miles of shoreline from Puʻu Kole Point to Paliuli, the sea cliff at the foot of Puʻuwai Village. Kaʻakuʻu is probably best known as Lehua Landing, the usual landing site for the Navy LCM (landing craft mechanized) that calls weekly at Niʻihau from Kauaʻi. The landing site is marked by a *kiawe*-post corral on the dunes behind the center of the beach. The boat is operated by Niʻihau Ranch and hauls livestock, equipment, passengers, food (including poi), dry goods, and other necessities to the island from Makaweli Landing on Kauaʻi.

Lehua Island, the landing's namesake, lies immediately off the northern end of the beach, barely three-fourths of a mile across the water. The crescent-shaped island is composed primarily of tuff, cemented volcanic ash. Other tuff cone islands in Hawaiʻi include Molokini, between Maui and Kahoʻolawe, and Kaʻula, 22 miles southwest of Niʻihau. Although Lehua Island has no beaches, landings are possible at several places where waves have cut benches into the base of the island. Seabirds are the only residents. During the winter, high surf pounds the island, climbing high up its northern and western faces. The winter months also see the arrival of many humpback whales and schools of dolphins, common not only in the waters around Lehua, but around the entire island of Niʻihau.

Kaʻakuʻu Beach is 0.75 mile long and averages 50 feet in width. It winds between Puʻu Kole and Kaunuokahe points. The backshore consists of low sand dunes 15 to

20 feet high, covered with *pōhinahina,* the dominant strand vegetation on the western side of the island. It is an attractive plant, with fragrant leaves and purple flowers, and an excellent groundcover on the hot dunes.

The rocky point at the northern end of Ka'aku'u Beach is marked by a stand of scrub ironwoods. The point extends into the ocean in an arc of small rock islets separated by waters averaging only 15 to 20 feet in depth. Seaward of the rock islets the shoals continue nearly a quarter-mile into the channel between Ni'ihau and Lehua Island. The beach is narrow at its northern end, but widens toward the south. At its southern end, it hooks out into the ocean, creating a natural trap for driftwood, fishing floats, bottles, shells, and other debris swept onshore during periods of high surf.

Almost the entire length of Ka'aku'u Beach is fronted by small patch reefs and rocky shoals. The exception is the shoreline fronting Lehua Landing, where the water offshore is deeper and a sand channel runs into the beach. Periods of high surf generate dangerous water conditions, particularly a strong shorebreak and powerful rip currents. Surf also breaks on many of the shallow offshore reefs.

KA'AKU'U. Ka'aku'u Bay, shown here above the dark, basaltic fingers of Kaunuokahe Point, is the site of Lehua Landing, the major landing on the island. The landing was named for its proximity to Lehua Island, which is just offshore. During the winter months when all landings are precluded by high surf striking this coast, the Ni'ihau Ranch boat from Pākalā, Kaua'i, stops at Ki'i Landing on the northeast coast to discharge its passengers and supplies.

KAʻAKUʻU. Kaʻakuʻu Beach is typical of Niʻihau's north shore beaches—long, white, and swept clean by high winter surf. *Pōhinahina* or beach vitex, an endemic Hawaiian coastal plant, grows profusely in the sand dunes here and in other dune complexes along the northwest and southwest coasts of the island. *Pōhinahina* is a low-lying shrub that blooms with blue or purplish flowers. Several small ironwood trees are visible at the north end of the beach.

Keawanui Beach

O Ka Mikioi. He makani pahele hala keia no Lehua, aole nui kona pa ana mai i ke kakahiaka no a mahana ae, pau no.

The Mikioi. This is a deceiving wind of Lehua Island. It does not blow very hard. It usually comes in the early morning. When it becomes warm, the wind disappears.

Ke Au Okoa
July 24, 1865

Keawanui appropriately means "the big bay." It is 3.5 miles long, the longest bay on Niʻihau. Keawanui Beach lines the entire bay and, with an average width of 175 feet, it is the largest beach on the island. Although the length of the beach remains constant, the sand is subject to seasonal erosion, and thus the width is reduced considerably during the winter months.

A continuous strip of vegetated sand dunes forms the backshore from Palikoaʻe to Kaununui Point. This extensive dune system varies in width from 100 yards at the northern end of the beach to 0.5 mile at the southern end, where the dunes reach heights of 100 feet above sea level. The dunes that line the backshore at Keawanui and nearly every other beach on the island play an important role in curbing the erosion of Niʻihau's shoreline. They serve as a flexible, but permanent, buffer between the ocean and the island.

The nearshore bottom bordering the northern half of the beach is for the most part sandy, and shallow sand bars form in many areas. During the winter, surf breaks on the sand bars, on many of the shallow offshore reefs, and at the rocky points such as Palikoa'e. High surf generates dangerous water conditions, particularly pounding shorebreaks, strong backwashes, and powerful rip currents.

The southern half of the beach is dominated by extensive sections of beachrock. The backshore in this area is covered with broken beachrock blocks and slabs, testimony to the force of the winter surf that strikes this shoreline. During the summer the bay is normally calm.

The winter surf that strikes the Hawaiian Islands is usually highest during the period from October to March, although it may begin as early as September and end as late as May. During the annual winter surf season, wave heights commonly reach 15 to 20 feet. As these tremendously powerful waves approach our beaches, they thoroughly scour the nearshore ocean bottom and the fringing reefs, picking up and carrying anything that is loose and unattached. When these waves finally sweep up on a beach, they deposit vast quantities of debris. In addition to all of the tiny organic and inorganic particles that constitute "sand," the debris includes seaweed, large fragments of coral, and a wide variety of shells. On Ni'ihau the shells are of particular interest to the residents of the island.

KEAWANUI. Immediately inland of Kaununui Point an extensive region of sand dunes, somewhat resembling the forward edge of a lava flow, appears to overrun the *kiawe* and other coastal vegetation. Pushed by high surf and strong winds, the sand masses are drifting north to south from Keawanui Beach toward Kauwaha Beach.

The people of Niʻihau collect shells to string into leis. The beautiful leis they fashion are among the few examples of pre-contact native Hawaiian artwork that are still made in Hawaiʻi today. The leis are made of tiny shells commonly called Niʻihau shells or *pupu Niʻihau*. Keawanui Beach is one of the chief collecting sites. The shells are also found on the island's other northeastern beaches to the north and south of Keawanui, and on several of the windward beaches.

The four species of shells most commonly referred to as Niʻihau shells are *Euptica varians* or *momi, Mitrella margarita* or *laiki, Leptothyra verruca* or *kahelelani,* and *Turbo sandwicensis* or *kamoa. Momi,* "pearl," are dove shells that have an oval shape. *Laiki,* "rice," resemble grains of rice and are usually strung in simple single strands. *Kahelelani,* "the royal going," the name of an ancient chief of Niʻihau, are small turban shells that come in a variety of colors. *Kamoa,* "the *moa* plant," are also turban shells whose spire tips resemble the yellow spores of their namesake plant. Contrary to popular belief, Niʻihau shells are found on the other Hawaiian islands, but they occur in much greater abundance on Niʻihau's beaches than elsewhere, and the quality of Niʻihau's shells is usually far superior.

Shell collecting takes place throughout the winter during and immediately after periods of high surf. In her book *Niʻihau Shell Leis,* the most authoritative work on the subject, author Linda Paik Moriarty describes the arduous task of collecting.

When a favorable site has been selected, the collectors assume a comfortable sitting or lying position on the debris line where most of the shells have accumulated. The collectors then move slowly along the debris line, repositioning themselves each time they have finished combing a particular area.

While the collectors are gathering shells, they do little or no talking to each other. They concentrate totally on the task at hand, focusing their eyes only on the shells. They move their eyes very slowly, an inch at a time. The constant focusing necessary to discern such tiny objects coupled with the harsh, intense glare of the sun reflecting on the sand and the ocean's surface puts a tremendous strain on the eyes.

The most determined collectors tolerate the long hours in the hot sun for an entire day, but most of them are not able to endure the harsh exposure and leave after four or five hours.

On an average day of collecting, one person may fill a small baby food jar [with shells].

A single lei requires hundreds of the tiny shells, so collecting and sorting by types, colors, and sizes is a never-ending job that continues from one winter season to the next. The quantity of shells needed to make a lei far exceeds the actual number of shells in the lei. Even the most skilled lei-makers break between 30 and 50 percent of their shells while piercing them for stringing. When a lei is eventually completed, a tremendous amount of time, effort, and painstaking attention to detail has been expended to produce an exquisite piece of fine jewelry. For this reason Niʻihau shell leis command very high prices and are an important source of income for the residents of the island.

Kauwaha Beach

O Ka Unulau. He makani ua keia no Niihau, ola ka wi nui o keia Mokupuni ke hiki mai ka ua, heaha la ia mea i ke keiki Unulau a Hina? Ke hooua mai, he ola, pa i Niihau, o na makani kaulana keia o Niihau nei a i hakuia hoi ma ke Mele a na haku Alii o kakou penei:

> *Eia mai ka Unulau malalo o Halalii,*
> *Lawe ke Koolau i ka hoa la lilo*
> *Hao ka mikioi i ke kai o Lehua,*
> *Pu-a wale ia no na hoa la-e!*

The Unulau. This is Niihau's rainy wind. Great famine is removed from this island when rain comes. It matters not to the Unulau child of Hina. [It is welcomed.] When it rains, life is blown to Niihau. These are the famous winds of Niihau to which meles were composed by our great alii composers thus:

The Unulau appears below Halalii.
The Koolau takes its companion [the sun] out of sight.
The Mikioi blows with great force to the sea of Lehua
    Island.
The companions are parted from me.

Ke Au Okoa
July 24, 1865

People who have never seen Niʻihau do not realize that most of the island is very dry and arid. With its highest

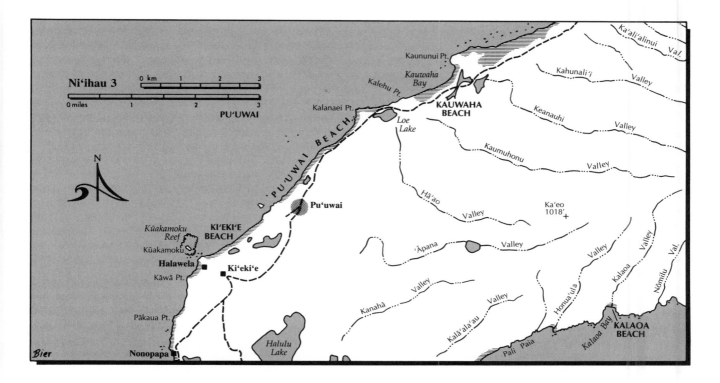

point only 1,281 feet above sea level, the 18-mile-long by 6-mile-wide island receives on the average only 12 inches of rain per year. By climatological definition any place that averages less than 10 inches of rain is a desert. Ni'ihau comes close.

Following extended periods of heavy rains, the island can be productive. Some eighteenth-century explorers, such as Nathaniel Portlock, found that the Hawaiians there were successfully cultivating large quantities of yams, in addition to sweet potatoes and sugar cane. Though he was able to replenish his provisions, Portlock advised that good drinking water was scarce and that ships visiting the island should seek it there only if they were in distress. Other foreign visitors to Ni'ihau were not as fortunate in securing provisions. In 1783 George Vancouver found that a prolonged period of severe drought had left the island barren and that most of the native residents had moved to Kaua'i.

The subsistence life-style on Ni'ihau, including periodic moves to Kaua'i during times of severe drought,

has always been harder than in other more fertile places in the islands. For this reason Ni'ihau has always had comparatively fewer permanent residents than the larger Hawaiian islands. Those who chose to tolerate the harsher conditions, however, were individualists who preferred the independence that their isolated home allowed them.

Today the people of Ni'ihau still maintain these traits of individualism and independence that have long been their heritage. That they have been able to do so is a result of the minimal contact they have had with the variety of cultures now so close to them. This limited exposure has been insured by the isolation of the island itself and by the policy of the owners of the island since 1864, the Robinson family of Kaua'i, to allow all of those born on Ni'ihau to live there for life and to provide them with work through Ni'ihau Ranch.

Ni'ihau residents have traditionally supplemented the food they purchase by fishing. Although the island has often been subjected to extended periods of barrenness, the ocean around it has always provided plenty of fish. In recent years, however, the fish populations have declined dramatically. Overfishing in the twentieth century has steadily diminished the fishing stocks around the heavily populated islands, and so commercial fishermen now frequent the waters surrounding Ni'ihau. These transient fishermen come primarily from Kaua'i, but also from O'ahu. This has caused concern among the island's owners and the Ni'ihau residents, who fear that one day their reefs may be as devoid of fish as those on O'ahu. A reduction in the residents' fish supply may diminish their capacity for self-sufficiency, an essential factor in keeping their unique native community intact.

Kauwaha Beach, one of the island's excellent fishing sites, extends for 2 miles between Kaununui Point and Kalanaei. Kaununui Point, a low rocky point backed by sand dunes, is fronted by a wide reef flat with several large tide pools. In the lee of the point, on its south side, a large sand-bottomed channel comes directly into the beach. Kauwaha beach consists of short sections of sand separated at the water's edge by beachrock and small rocky points. To the rear of the beach, vegetated sand dunes between 40 and 60 feet high extend several hundred yards inland.

During the winter, surf breaks on many of the shallow nearshore reefs and off the rocky points. Periods of high surf generate dangerous water conditions, particularly powerful rip currents. During the summer, the nearshore waters are normally calm.

Pu'uwai Beach

O Ka Papaainuwai. He makani malie keia, he hiki ke holo i Waimea, a me Hanalei, Kauai, a pela no hoi ko Kauai mai, he hiki no ke holo mai i Niihau nei. Elua na ano o keia makani, i kekahi wa, he Papaainuwai, a he ua

Pu'uwai. Approximately 200 people, the majority of them native Hawaiians, live in Pu'uwai, the only inhabited village site on Ni'ihau. Hawaiian is spoken as a first language in the village, one of the last places in Hawai'i where this still occurs. In addition to walking, the residents transport themselves primarily by riding horses and bicycles.

kehau ke ano, a o kekahi hoi me he makani la, nolaila i kapaia ai he Papaala, he la i oi aku mamua o Kuakaha, i Hana, Maui Hikina.

The Papaainuwai. This wind is calm so that one is able to sail to Waimea and Hanalei, Kauai, and likewise, those of Kauai can sail here to Niihau. There are two characteristics of this wind. Sometimes it is Papaainuwainui which is misty rain and at other times it is like true rain. Therefore it is also named Papaala in which the heat surpasses that of Kuakaha at Hana, East Maui.

Ke Au Okoa
July 24, 1865

Pu'uwai, meaning "heart," is the name of the only inhabited village on Ni'ihau. Approximately 200 people, most of them native Hawaiians, live at Pu'uwai. The entire island is operated as Ni'ihau Ranch by the Robinson family of Makaweli, Kaua'i, and most of Pu'uwai's residents are employees of the ranch or their families. The ranch provides them with wood-frame houses, modest salaries, and medical insurance, and insures that their domestic and health needs are met. As ranch employees, the residents tend herds of cattle and sheep, make charcoal from *kiawe* wood, and collect honey. They also fish and pick *'opihi,* although these resources have been severely taxed by off-island commercial fishermen.

The rural life-style at Pu'uwai is very simple. There are no telephones, no electricity, and no alcoholic beverages. Rainwater is caught and stored in cisterns for drinking. If the cisterns go dry, water is hauled from shallow wells. The primary means of transportation are walking and riding bicycles or horses. Children attend Ni'ihau School through the eighth grade and then transfer to Waimea High School on Kaua'i. Everyone attends the Congregational church, the only church in the village. A radio transmitter is used to call Kaua'i in case of emergencies. Obviously, the owners of the island and the residents have elected to embrace only a minimum of the offerings of the modern society that surrounds them.

The private ownership of Ni'ihau dates back to the 1860s. In September 1863, the barque *Bessie* arrived in Honolulu from New Zealand carrying thirteen family members named either Robinson, Gay, or Sinclair. Successful farmers in New Zealand, they had sold their holdings and had come to Hawai'i in search of greater opportunities. The matriarch of the clan was Elizabeth McHutchison Sinclair, the Scottish widow of a sea captain. King Kamehameha IV felt that she and her extended family would be an asset to the islands. He offered to sell Ni'ihau to her if she would remain in Hawai'i. Mrs. Sinclair accepted his offer and purchased the entire island for $10,000 cash. The king died while the sale was being transacted, and so title was conveyed to Mrs. Sinclair by Lot Kamehameha, King Kamehameha V, on January 23, 1864.

In later years, Mrs. Sinclair purchased the 21,844-acre *ahupua'a* of Makaweli and other large tracts of land on Kaua'i. Today, Makaweli is the headquarters of the family's extensive Kaua'i holdings, which include Makaweli Ranch, Olokele Sugar Mill, and the Gay and Robinson Sugar Company, as well as the island of Ni'ihau. When Mrs. Sinclair purchased the island in 1864, she asked her son Francis to manage it. This he did until 1883, when Aubrey Robinson, his nephew, the son of his sister Helen Robinson, took over. It was Aubrey who brought to an end an era of hospitality that had seen regular stops by the interisland steamships and reception of many visitors and summer guests at the family's large home at Ki'eki'e. In the wake of the acquisition of the Hawaiian Islands as a territory of the United States in 1898, Aubrey made a decision to preserve the Hawaiian language and culture on Ni'ihau by severely restricting access to the island. By 1915 the isolation had been effected, and no one was allowed to visit Ni'ihau, including relatives of the Hawaiians living there, without his personal permission.

Management of Ni'ihau Ranch was assumed by Aubrey Robinson's oldest son, Aylmer, in 1922. In 1927 Aylmer brought his youngest brother Lester on board to serve as assistant manager. Together the two of them continued their father's policies.

Aylmer died a bachelor in 1968, leaving his interests in the island to his brother Lester and Lester's sons, Bruce and Keith Robinson. When Lester died shortly afterward, in October 1969, all of the interests in Ni'ihau were vested in his wife Helen and in Bruce and Keith, the present owners.

Since about the turn of the century, Ni'ihau has acquired an aura of mystery to the rest of the world. The main reason is the Robinson family's strict closed-door policy to all visitors, forbidding entry to anyone who is not a resident of the island, a member of the Robinson family, or an invited guest of the family. This policy extends also to virtually all inquiries about the island, the majority of which simply go unanswered.

With great determination the Robinsons protect their private property ownership rights. Trespassers on the island are commonly placed under citizen's arrest and then transported to Kaua'i at the earliest opportunity, where they are turned over to the county police. The off-limits policy is also extended to boaters who come ashore to beachcomb. They are told to return to their boats, an action that raises an interesting legal question. Are the beaches on Ni'ihau public or private? In 1973 a landmark ruling on Hawaiian beaches by the Hawai'i State Supreme Court set the shoreline boundary between public and private property at the vegetation line. In 1985 this decision was further refined by the passage of Act 104, which defines the public shoreline as extending inland "to the upper reaches of the wash of waves, usually evidenced by the edge of vegetation growth or by the upper limit of debris left by the wash of the waves." These legislative acts make it very clear that all beaches in the Hawaiian Islands are public property up to the vegetation line.

Ni'ihau's owners, however, believe that their deed gives them title to the beach as well as the land above it. In an article in the *Honolulu Advertiser* on public access, dated October 29, 1988, Bruce Robinson stated, "Our deed very clearly leads to the water. It is a separate deed quite unique in Hawaii. It stems directly from the monarchy, and with it comes the aboriginal rights of the old days." To date, the Robinsons' claims of private beach ownership have not been challenged by anyone who has been asked to leave the island. Undoubtedly, most visitors to Ni'ihau's beaches respect the Robinsons' long-standing ownership of the island and their obvious desire for privacy. People in Hawai'i are aware that Ni'ihau is a special place.

Author Ruth Tabrah has expressed Ni'ihau's uniqueness in the title of her comprehensive historical account of the island—*Ni'ihau, The Last Hawaiian Island.* Without help from any public or private sources, the Robinson family has made Ni'ihau the last truly Hawaiian island by preserving as much as possible of the native culture. Of course, many compromises have been made with contemporary society in the matters of clothing, domestic needs, ranch equipment, and some amenities, but none in the traditions, and especially none in the language. The Robinsons have long recognized that language is the essence of culture. Ni'ihau remains the last place in Hawai'i where Hawaiian is spoken exclusively as a first language in daily life.

The Robinsons and the Ni'ihau residents continue to speak the Hawaiian dialect that Captain Cook found so similar to Tahitian. To other native Hawaiian speakers, the Ni'ihau dialect is very distinct, with many sounds that are different from standard Hawaiian. Most noticeable is the frequent use of *t* for *k. Kakou,* for example, the pronoun for "all of us," is *katou;* the word for spider is *tutuati'i.* Dialectic differences aside, the point of importance is that Hawaiian on Ni'ihau is a living language. It remains an unbroken link to pre-contact Hawaiian society and at the same time continues to evolve with exposure to modern society, limited as that is. *Sila,* for example, is Ni'ihau's Hawaiianized version of the word *seal,* while *kūhoe* is a brand new word for the fin of a surfboard.

In the September 1878 issue of *The Friend,* the Reverend Lorenzo Lyons wrote:

> I've studied Hawaiian for 46 years but am by no means perfect. . . . It is an interminable language . . . one of the oldest living languages of earth, as some conjecture, and may well be classed among the best. . . . The thought to displace it, or to doom it to oblivion by substituting the English language, ought not for a moment to be indulged. Long live the grand old, sonorous, poetical Hawaiian language.

In her book on Ni'ihau, Ruth Tabrah notes that there has always been a great deal of conjecture that someday the island might change, especially with the passing of each Robinson generation. She writes the following about the questions that arose after the death of Lester Robinson:

> The family shunted off recurring rumors and speculation as to what might happen in the near future by stating, "too much of a mystery has been made of the Ni'ihau operation. It is simply a ranching operation and

it would be disruptive to permit visitors who would come out of curiosity." "Those interested in the past," proclaimed an editorial in the Advertiser, "will be encouraged to know that Lester Robinson passed on to his sons Bruce and Keith his feelings for the island and its status as something removed from time."

Pu'uwai Beach is a narrow, continuous sandy stretch, extending for 2 miles from Kalanaei to Paliuli. Low, vegetated dunes form the backshore. Basalt boulders are scattered in the beach's foreshore immediately north of Paliuli. During the winter, surf breaks on many of the shallow nearshore reefs and off the rocky points such as Paliuli. High surf generates dangerous water conditions, particularly powerful rip currents. During the summer, the nearshore waters are normally calm.

Paliuli is the most dominant feature on the shoreline. It is a massive point of basalt that is bisected into twin sea cliffs by a small pocket of sand. The black lava contrasts very dramatically with the long white sand

KI'EKI'E. Kūakamoku Reef lies offshore Ki'eki'e Beach while inland of the beach are the headquarters of Ni'ihau Ranch. Rooftops of some of the homes in Pu'uwai Village are barely visible as white dots at the north end of the beach. The sand terminates at Paliuli, twin basalt sea cliffs below the village.

91

beaches on either side. The village of Pu'uwai is located immediately inland of Paliuli. Many large trees shelter the homes in this shoreline community.

Ki'eki'e Beach

O Ke Kiu. He makani anu loa keia, ma Kauai mai a noho i Niihau nei, ua like pu no kakou i kana hana, oia hoi, e loku ana ka io i ke anu a ke Kiu.

The Kiu. A very cold wind [that blows] from Kauai and settles on Niihau. We have experienced its action which is to feel deep emotion. [It] blows as a gale, very cold-tempered.

Ke Au Okoa
July 24, 1865

When Elizabeth Sinclair and her family purchased Ni'ihau, it was their intention not only to establish a cattle and sheep ranch there, but to make the island their home. By spring of that year, they had moved from Honolulu and were living temporarily in grass houses at Pu'uwai. For their permanent home, they selected a site on a rise at Ki'eki'e that commanded excellent views of the ocean and the rest of the island. The Ki'eki'e home was completed and the family had moved in by the end of the year. Within a few years, however, Mrs. Sinclair and most of the family members decided to live on Kaua'i and moved to the family's extensive land holdings at Makaweli. The home at Ki'eki'e continued to serve as the family's Ni'ihau headquarters and as the center of ranch operations on the island.

Ki'eki'e Beach is one of the two major beaches on the southwestern side of the island. It curves for 1.25 miles between Paliuli and Halawela. During the summer, the beach widens to 175 feet, whereas during the winter, high surf erodes the shoreline, reducing the volume of sand onshore. The sandy foreshore slopes steeply into the ocean and is occasionally interrupted by sections of beachrock. The bottom drops quickly to overhead depths near the shore. Dangerous water conditions occur during periods of high surf, particularly a pounding shorebreak, strong backwashes, and powerful rip currents. During the summer, the ocean is normally calm. In the backshore, low dunes extend several hundred yards inland.

A series of small rock islets and sea stacks project offshore of the southern end of the beach. The largest islet is 1.1-acre Kuakamoku. The sea stacks are submerged, but even during periods of calm seas a line of whitewater is normally visible to mark their location.

Nonopapa Beach

O Ka Aoa. He makani ikaika no keia, he makani kaulana keia mai Hanapepe, Kauai mai, he makani waiwai no makou o Niihau nei, mai kou hiki malihini ana mai a hiki i keia wa, he makani waapa nui no na keiki o Kapahee, he makani haehae lole no Nonopapa a me Kamalino, kala no hoi, a uhi wale lole no hoi.

The Aoa. It is a strong wind. It is a famous wind that blows from Hanapepe, Kauai. It is an important wind for us here at Niihau. Since my arrival here as a stranger, to this day this wind has been [good] for [sailing] children's large boats at Kapahee. However, it tears clothing [off the line] at Nonopapa and Kamalino, tears up money, just overwhelming clothes.

Ke Au Okoa
July 24, 1865

In January 1778, Captain James Cook, the British commander of a voyage of exploration in the Pacific, made the first recorded visit by a Westerner to the Hawaiian Islands. He landed first at Waimea on Kaua'i. After provisioning his two ships with food and water, he set out to explore Ni'ihau. On January 29, he and his men dropped anchor off the rocky shoreline immediately south of Kamalino, the site of a small village.

After Cook's death on February 14, 1779, at Ka'awaloa on the Big Island, James King assumed command of the expedition. In search of provisions once again, King eventually put into Ni'ihau and anchored in the same area near Kamalino. A heavy easterly swell was running, making the anchorage difficult, so King moved his ships farther north to Nonopapa. There, in addition to another small village, they found a long sandy beach, deep nearshore waters, an extensive reservoir of sand at anchoring depths, and a small rocky point at the north end of the beach that offered some protection to boats going ashore, even during periods of moderately high surf.

King's anchorage at Nonopapa was revisited in 1786 by Captains Nathaniel Portlock and George Dixon,

92

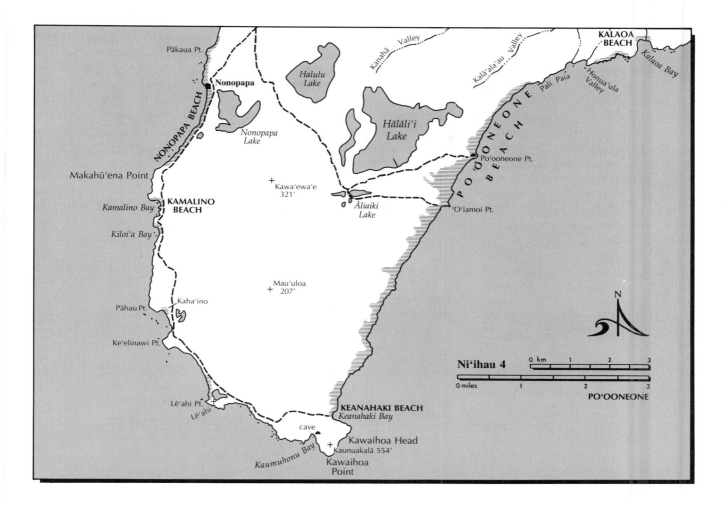

Ni'ihau 4

PO'OONEONE

both of whom had been with Cook and King. In spite of Ni'ihau's dry and desolate appearance, the native Hawaiians there grew yams in abundance, and Portlock and Dixon were able to take on some water and a large quantity of yams. They christened the anchorage Yam Bay.

Late in the eighteenth century, Yam Bay was visited by a number of other sailing ships looking for provisions. The approach to Ni'ihau was apparently always the same, as the vessels navigated around Kawaihoa, the southern tip of the island, and then headed up the southwestern coast in the lee of the island until they reached Nonopapa.

During the nineteenth century, Yam Bay became known as Nonopapa Landing. In the latter part of the century, it was used occasionally as an interisland steamer landing. Today, Nonopapa is marked by a large green corrugated iron warehouse, several *kiawe*-post corrals, and a stand of coconut trees. Kawa'ewa'e Hill, a large cinder cone 290 feet high, dominates the view immediately inland.

Nonopapa is described in "Kawaihoa," a traditional Ni'ihau song.

O 'ike 'ia o ka 'aina	Well known in this land
A o Nonopapa	Is Nonopapa
Ke kai ho'omalie	Where the sea is soothing
Ka nani ho'ohenoheno.	With a caressing beauty.

93

NONOPAPA. A lone warehouse adjoins several corrals at the north end of Nonopapa Beach. In former times Nonopapa was used as a landing by ships sailing around Kawaihoa, the southern tip of the island. Nonopapa, like Lehua Landing to the north, is subject to high surf during the winter and spring.

Nonopapa Beach is the second of the two major beaches on the southwestern side of the island. It curves for 2 miles between Nonopapa and Makahuʻena points. In the backshore, sand dunes 15 to 20 feet high are covered with *pōhinahina* and extend several hundred yards inland. During the summer, when the ocean is normally calm, the width of the beach varies from 50 feet at the north end to 125 feet at its southern extremity. During the winter, high surf erodes the shoreline, reducing the volume of sand onshore. The sandy foreshore slopes steeply into the ocean and is occasionally interrupted by beachrock and small clusters of boulders. The bottom drops quickly to overhead depths near shore. Periods of high surf generate dangerous water conditions, particularly a pounding shorebreak, strong backwashes, and powerful rip currents. During the winter, surf breaks offshore of the warehouse at the northern point of the beach. When winter surf is particularly high, waves 20 feet and higher break between 1 and 1.5 miles offshore on shoaling reefs.

Kamalino Beach

O Ke Kona. He makani keia i papalua ia kona ano ma Niihau nei, he Kona, a he Konaelua, he makani ikaika keia mai ke Komohana Hema mai, ua kamaaina kakou i kona ano, hele mai ka ua me ka makani, kelekele na ala-nui, holomoku na wai kahe, ku ke oka wahie aia i kai, kau ke alapii o ka Oopu, aia iloko o ka mawae o na pohaku a me na kipona lepo, a pela aku.

The Kona. This is a wind that hits twice as hard here on Niihau. It is a Kona and it is also a double Kona. It is a strong wind from the southwest. We are familiar with its characteristics. The rain comes in with the wind, the road

94

becomes muddy, water flows and is almost fit to sail in; much debris is left on the beaches; step formations are created for the oopu fish to climb up, situated within the spaces of the rocks and soil banks, and so on.

Ke Au Okoa
July 24, 1865

Kamalino is a small bay on Ni'ihau's rocky southwestern shore that was once the site of a small Hawaiian fishing village. During the twentieth century several wooden houses were built in the area and used by Ni'ihau ranch hands, but these were abandoned during the 1930s. Today, Kamalino is marked only by a small pocket of sand tucked into the corner of the bay. On clear days, the small island of Ka'ula is visible on the horizon 22 miles to the west. Both Ka'ula and Kamalino are mentioned in "Kawaihoa," a traditional Ni'ihau song:

He nani a o Ka'ula	Beautiful is Ka'ula Island
'Āina o nā manu	Land of many birds
Ke kai ho'o'olu ana	Refreshing is the ocean
A o Kamalino.	At Kamalino.

During periods of high surf, waves break at the northern point of the bay and at several other points to the south. One of these points is known to some boaters as Antennas. The "antennas" are the radio towers of the former Ni'ihau Loran station, a communication facility that was built in 1944, during World War II. The station with its control building and living quarters was decommissioned and abandoned in 1951.

The people of Ni'ihau knew the station as Waiū and composed a song in its honor called "Po'e Koa o Ni'ihau," the "Soldiers of Ni'ihau":

Aloha ka po'e koa a o Ni'ihau	Aloha soldiers of Ni'ihau
Noho ana i ka uluwehi	Living in the beauty
Ka poli a o Waiū.	In the heart of Waiū.
Eia mākou ke kia'i nei	We are here guarding
No ka polo o ke aupuni	To protect the country
A o Alelika.	Of America.
Ho'oholo mai 'oe i kahe likini	You start the radio

No ke kahea ana aku I Kaua'i.	For the daily call To Kaua'i.
Ha'ina 'ia mai ana ka puana	Tell the refrain again
Noho ana i ka uluwehi	Living in the beauty
Ka po'e a o Waiū.	The soldiers at Waiū.

Low sea cliffs form the shoreline from Kamalino to Kawaihoa, the southern tip of the island. Small pockets of sand, sections of beachrock, and basalt boulders lie at the base of the cliffs. Although *kiawe* is the dominant coastal plant, this end of the island is noted for another type of strand vegetation, *pilo. Pilo,* which is also known as *puapilo* and *maiapilo,* is the Hawaiian caper, famed for its fragrant, delicate, many-stamened flowers. In *Ni'ihau, the Last Hawaiian Island,* author Ruth Tabrah notes that Captain Cook went ashore at this end of the island and walked some distance to the north. He probably encountered the low-branching bushes of *pilo* because he reported the following in his journal: "The ground through which I passed was in a state of nature, very strong, and the soil seemed poor. It was, however, covered with shrubs and plants, some of which perfumed the air with a more delicious fragrance than I had met with at any of the other islands visited by us in this ocean."

Kawaihoa, the southern tip of the island is a massive, solitary hill that stands 550 feet high. Boaters commonly call it South Point. Two miles back up the southwestern coast, a smaller hill called Lē'ahi sits on a rocky point. The names of these two sites are the same as the names of two similar sites on O'ahu, Lē'ahi (Diamond Head) and Kawaihoa (Koko Head). There are a number of interesting similarities between these two pairs of places bearing identical names, including their locations on the southeastern ends of the islands, their locations on the shoreline in relation to each other, the narrow sand beaches that lie at their bases, and their offshore wind-shear lines during normal trade winds. The most striking similarities, however, are in the two Kawaihoa's. Both of these headlands are huge, rounded, brown, volcanic cones made of tuff, or volcanic ash, cemented into firm rock. Both of them contain blocks of older volcanic rocks and limestone from the coral reefs that were torn apart during the explosions that built them. Both

95

of them exhibit fretwork created by the constant weathering of sea spray in the soft, thin-bedded tuff on their faces. Both of them have wave-cut sea caves and wave-cut benches along their bases. The resemblances are very strong.

Tuff eruptions are younger geologically than the basalt rocks upon which they are built, and they provide Hawai'i with some of its most singular landmarks. Kawaihoa on Ni'ihau is no exception; it is one of the unique geographic features on the island. The residents of Ni'ihau have a great deal of aloha for the mountain and tell of its beauty in the song "Kawaihoa." The following is the song's first verse:

Kaulana mai nei	Famous throughout Hawai'i is
Ka lani o Kawaihoa	The majesty of Kawaihoa
Ka lani a o Lē'ahi	And the majesty of Lē'ahi
Ka beauty a o Ni'ihau.	The beautiful places of Ni'ihau.

Keanahaki Beach

O Ka Aoalaenihi. He makani ua keia, ma Nihi mai, oia ka mea i kapaia ai e ka poe kahiko, he Aoalaenihi, no kona hele nihi ana mai.

The Aoalaenihi. This is a windy rain from Nihi which is why the ancients named it Aoalaenihi. It moves quietly.

Ke Au Okoa
July 24, 1865

Kawaihoa, the massive tuff cone that makes up the southern tip of Ni'ihau, is exposed to the open ocean on three sides. The erosive forces of trade winds, high surf, and heavy storms have eroded two deep bays on either side of it.

One bay, Kaumuhonu, is located on the western side in the lee of the point. It is used as an anchorage during normal trade wind weather, but during periods of *kona*, or southerly, storms, and summer periods of southerly

KAWAIHOA. Kawaihoa, known to boaters as South Point, rises over 500 feet above the ocean at the southern tip of Ni'ihau. This massive headland consists largely of tuff—consolidated volcanic ash—and in structure closely resembles Koko Head on O'ahu. High surf has eroded the tuff to form Kaumuhonu Bay, visible here below the western face of the cone.

96

PO'OONEONE. Po'ooneone, a 50-foot high headland on the southeastern side of the island, is a prominant coastal landmark. Po'ooneone means "sandy head," an appropriate name for this isolated point made of lithified sand dunes (eolianite) and covered with a thin veneer of sand. The row of sand mounds in the foreground marks the hole-digging efforts of 'ōhiki, common Hawaiian sand crabs, that come ashore at night.

swell, it is exposed to high surf. The Kaumuhonu shoreline is primarily a tuff sea cliff with a small detrital storm beach overlying a low bench at the head of the bay.

The second bay, Keanahaki, is located to windward on the eastern side of Kawaihoa. It is used as an anchorage during *kona* storms and during periods of calm seas. It is a much shallower bay than Kaumuhonu, with nearshore water depths of 6 to 8 feet. A large pocket of sand fronted by a low rocky shelf lines the head of the bay. A wave-cut basalt bench extends the length of the bay to a point that hooks out into the ocean. The hook makes the bay a natural trap for driftwood, fishing floats, bottles, shells, nets, and other debris commonly swept onshore by the trade winds and high surf.

Keanahaki was formerly a popular summer retreat for the Robinsons and their guests. Several grass houses and a small wooden cottage once stood on the low sea cliffs above the beach. Only the house foundations remain today. Keanahaki is also the second of two landing sites on the island for Ni'ihau Helicopters Inc., an air tour service, owned and operated by Ni'ihau Ranch, that was started in June 1987. The tours originate on Kaua'i, make two stops on Ni'ihau, and then return to Kaua'i. The first stop is at Kamakalepo Point at the northern tip of the island. In addition to the tours, the helicopter is used to transport family members and employees between Kaua'i and Ni'ihau and to take Ni'ihau residents to Kaua'i during medical emergencies.

Po'ooneone Beach

O Ke Koolau. He makani lewe mai keia i ke ahi me ka pulupulu, ua like keia makani me ka Ilio hae la, ka hele a hanupanupa ka moana, i kahele huhu a keiki o na pali Koolau.

The Koolau. This is the wind that carries away the sparks of fire kindling. This wind is like a barking dog, when it comes the ocean is choppy like an angry child along the Koolau cliffs.

Ke Au Okoa
July 24, 1865

Po'ooneone Beach extends for 2.5 miles from 'O'iamoi Point to the sea cliffs at Pā'ia. It is the only major beach on the southeastern side of the island. Po'ooneone Point, the 50-foot-high headland for which the beach is named, bisects this long stretch of shoreline. Po'ooneone means "sandy head," an appropriate name for this isolated landmark standing at the water's edge. It is made of lithified sand dunes (eolianite) with a thin veneer of sand.

PO'OONEONE. Po'ooneone Beach is a beachcomber's paradise. It faces into the prevailing trade winds, making it a receptacle for every piece of debris pushed shoreward by the wind, waves, and currents. Japanese fishing floats, highly prized by Hawai'i's beachcombers and popularly known as "glass balls," are often found in these large pockets of litter.

98

The mile-long stretch of sand from 'O'iamoi to Po'ooneone points averages 100 feet in width. It is lined by low, wide sections of beachrock. Incoming surf sweeping over and around it has eroded a series of tidal pools in the sand between the sections of beach rock. Driftwood, fishing floats, bottles, shells, and other debris litter the entire beach, but tend to concentrate near Po'ooneone Point. Low extensive sand dunes slope inland for 1.5 miles to Lake Hālāli'i, a shallow, intermittent lake. *Kiawe* is the primary strand vegetation.

On the north side of Po'ooneone Point, the beach continues for 1.5 miles to Pā'ia. This section of shoreline is also fronted with wide, raised sections of beachrock and tidal pools that parallel the beachrock. An especially large, circular, sand-bottomed pool is located in the lee of the point. Elsewhere, the beachrock outcrops are bisected in several places by narrow sand channels that run into the beach. Driftwood, fishing floats, bottles, shells, and other debris litter the entire beach, but tend to concentrate in the areas near the sand channels and where the sections of beachrock are low and flat. The steep, sparsely vegetated sand dunes to the rear of the beach are 20 to 30 feet high.

As one of the two major windward beaches on the island, Po'ooneone, like Pōleho to the north, is exposed directly to the trade winds and the constant surf that they generate. Waves break almost continually against the long sections of beachrock that line the beach. Small local rip currents are common in the surge channels among the rocks. Periods of calm seas prevail primarily during *kona* weather, when the wind is from the south or when there is no wind at all.

Kalaoa Beach

O Ke Kulepe. He makani pili aina ole mai keia, i ka moana wale iho no ia e lauwili ai, o kana hana , o ke kulepe i na waa holo mai Niihau aku, a pela no hoi mai Kauai mai.

The Kulepe. This wind does not touch land. It twists and turns only over the ocean, that is all it does, overturning canoes leaving Niihau or arriving from Kauai.

Ke Au Okoa
July 24, 1865

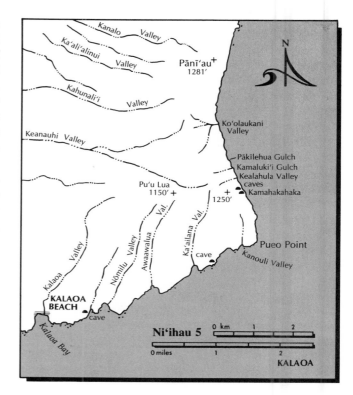

Much of the island of Ni'ihau is the remnant of a shield volcano. The northeastern edge of the remnant lies between Pueo Point, the eastern point of the island, and Pōleho Beach. High sea cliffs line this coastline and contain the highest point on the island, Pānī'au, at 1,281 feet. The southeastern edge of the remnant lies between Pueo Point and Po'ooneone Beach. The sea cliffs here are lower and are notched by a series of small, stream-cut valleys. Pockets of sand are found at the heads of several valleys, including Honua'ula, Kalaoa, and Nōmilu. The remainder, including 'Awa'awalua, Ka'ailana, and Kanouli, have small cobble and boulder beaches.

The most prominent valley of the series is Kalaoa. It is fronted by a wide pocket of sand, a barrier beach between Kalaoa Bay and intermittent Kalaoa Stream. When the stream flows after heavy rains, it carries large quantities of soil to the coastal waters, and it is common to see a wide plume of murky water flowing past the

KALAOA. The southeastern sea cliffs from Paia to Pueo Point are cut by a series of narrow coastal valleys, some of which contain small pocket beaches. Kalaoa Beach, the largest of the pocket beaches, is often fronted by a mud plume after heavy rains. Muddy water flowing down the valley overruns the beach, inundating the shorebreak and the small bay offshore.

south point of the bay. The sand in the backshore is heavily veneered with mud. A *muliwai,* a pond of brackish water, forms occasionally in the backshore. *Kiawe* is the dominant vegetation at the shoreline and in the narrow valley immediately inland.

The nearshore waters at Kalaoa Beach are dominated by a shallow sand bar paralleling the length of the beach. Tradewind-generated surf creates a typical windward beach break on the sand bar. Driftwood, fishing floats, and other wind-blown debris are found onshore, but in much smaller quantities than on the beaches at Pōleho, Po'ooneone, and Keanahaki.

Pōleho Beach

O Ke Kiulehua. He makani anuanu nui loa keia, no ka awili pu o ka Lehua me ke Kiu, oia ka mea i nui ai ke anu, aia keia makani ma ka Akau Hikina, hookahi no waiwai a keia makani, he anu, pupuu na hua i ke anu a ke Kiulehua.

Oia na inoa o na makani o ka Mokupuni holookoa o Niihau nei. Ua pau, a ke hoi nei ko Niihau keiki, ua kau iho la ka olu i ka ulu hala o Halawela. Me ke aloha no.

The Kiulehua. This is a very cold wind which is a combination of the Lehua and the Kiu winds which is the reason that it produces extreme coldness. This wind is located to the northeast. One important mention of this wind—because of its extreme coldness, it produces chill bumps upon the fruits [an exaggeration, of course, but an example of an individual's creativeness when describing something to make it sound more interesting].

These, then, are the winds of the entire island of Niihau. The descriptions are finished and Niihau's son is returning home [in other words, it is time to say goodbye]. Peace and quiet have settled upon the hala grove of Halawela. Affectionately,

P. P. Holi
Halawela, Niihau
Ke Au Okoa
July 24, 1865

Pōleho Beach is a 2.5-mile stretch of shoreline that extends from Ka'ali Cliff to Ki'i Landing. The only sand beach on the northeast shore of Ni'ihau, it averages 150 feet in width and is backed by low vegetated dunes. *Kiawe* predominates in the shoreline vegetation. Although the beach is interrupted by a series of small, low, rocky points, there are several wide, rock-free expanses between the points. These sites are exposed directly to the assault of the open ocean, and the dunes extend much farther inland than at the other areas along the shoreline. The largest rock-free section is at Pōleho, where the dunes are between 50 and 100 feet high and extend hundreds of feet inland into the base of Ka'ali Cliff. On a clear day, this broad expanse of unvegetated dunes is visible even from the road to Waimea Canyon on Kaua'i.

Pōleho Beach faces directly into the path of the trade winds. The beach is littered with masses of windblown debris, including driftwood, fishing floats, nets, and bottles. Cowrie shells are also common. The wind also generates a continual shorebreak on a shallow, sloping

PŌLEHO. The prevailing tradewinds have created an extensive series of sand dunes at Pōleho Beach, the only beach on Ni'ihau's northeast shore. This wide swath of unvegetated sand is even visible from Kaua'i on the road to Waimea Canyon, an elevated vantage point. The northern half of Lehua Island can be seen over the sand dunes and the adjoining *kiawe* forest.

PŌLEHO. Pōleho Beach is a typical Hawaiian windward beach. The constant blowing of the trade winds creates choppy, wind-blown surf that breaks on the shallow sandbars in its nearshore waters. The island of Kaua'i, visible across the Kaulakahi Channel, is 17 miles away.

sand bar near shore. Local rip currents are common during periods of high surf.

Ki'i Landing, located at the northern end of the beach, is marked by a shack and a corral. It is an alternate landing site for the Navy LCM (landing craft mechanized) operated by Ni'ihau Ranch. The boat calls weekly at the island to bring supplies for the residents. Ki'i Landing is used when high surf precludes the use of Lehua Landing at Ka'aku'u Beach. Even during periods of extremely high winter surf, Ki'i almost always offers a safe anchorage in the lee of Kaunuopou Point. Hawaiian monk seals seem to favor these calmer waters during the winter and are commonly sighted in the area. Seals are also seen around the northern end of the island at Pu'u Kole and Lehua Island, and at the southern end at Nonopapa, Kamalino, and Keanahaki.

In 1923 William Hyde Rice offered this explanation for the naming of Ki'i in his book *Hawaiian Legends:*

The people of the islands of Kauai and Niihau were accustomed to going to one end of Niihau to fish. But it often happened that while they were sleeping on the sand after a hard day's fishing, the akuas would come and devour many of the men.

At last one brave man declared that he would destroy the akuas and rid the island of this danger. So he built a longhouse, similar to a canoe house, leaving only one entrance. Then he made many kiis, or wooden images of people, placing in the heads mottled gray and black eyes of 'opihi, or mussel, shell. These images he put in the house, concealing himself outside.

At night the akuas began to come for their usual meal. Looking into the house they saw the kiis with their shining eyes. At first this surprised them, but as the images lay very still, the akuas decided that the Kauai men slept with their eyes open, and so they entered and tried to eat the images, with dire results. Their teeth were caught in the wood, and while they were struggling to free them, the crafty Kauai man quickly shut the door and set fire to the house, and all the cruel akuas were burned to death.

Thereafter Niihau became safe for fishermen, and this part of the island still bears the name Kii.

102

Water Safety

Dangerous Water Conditions

The longest and widest beaches on Kaua'i are located on the north and west shores. These beaches are not well protected by coral reefs, points of land, or other natural barriers. For this reason strong currents and other hazardous water conditions are present in many nearshore locations. Visitors unfamiliar with the ocean should be aware of such hazards as dangerous shorebreak waves and fast-flowing rip currents that are not found in lakes and streams or at other protected beaches.

Although a few of the popular county beach parks are served by lifeguards, most of the island's beaches are not. If you get into trouble in the ocean, help will probably be a long time coming unless someone happens to be nearby who is capable of assisting you. Avoid endangering yourself by reading about the beach you wish to visit, or by talking to a lifeguard, a beach attendant, or a local resident.

All beach users, especially those unfamiliar with island waters, should be able to recognize dangerous water conditions, especially shorebreaks, rip currents, and undertows.

Shorebreaks

Shorebreaks are places where waves break close to or directly on shore. Shorebreak waves from 1 to 3 feet high generally pose little threat to adults and usually provide good bodysurfing and bodyboarding opportunities. Shorebreak waves of 4 feet or higher, however, present some major hazards. These larger waves break with considerable downward force and often slam inex-

perienced swimmers onto the ocean bottom. Swimmers may suffer loss of breath, disorientation, or even injury, and any person temporarily incapacitated in the surf is a potential drowning candidate. As a general rule, any waves that are waist high or higher on any individual, either an adult or child, should be considered dangerous.

The majority of the near-drownings, drownings, ocean rescues, and ocean-related injuries on Kaua'i occur at shorebreak sites. Popular, unguarded shorebreak beaches such as Keālia, Lumaha'i, Hanakāpī'ai, Kalalau, and Polihale should be approached with a great deal of caution, especially during the winter and spring high surf season. Visitors should be aware that drowning victims have included not only swimmers, but also sightseers who have ventured too close to high surf sweeping across a beach or over the rocky margins of a bay. Invariably, these individuals have been caught off-guard by an unexpectedly large wave, swept off the beach or rocks into the high surf, and drowned.

Rip Currents

The word *rip* in this term is thought to be an abbreviated form of *riparian,* which means riverlike. Rip currents are narrow, fast-flowing, riverlike currents of water that travel from shallow, nearshore areas out to sea. They are generated primarily by surf and are commonly found wherever waves are breaking. When sets of incoming waves move large volumes of water into nearshore areas, the accumulated water begins to flow alongshore until it finds a break in the surf or a break in the reef. Then it rushes seaward into the open ocean, forming a rip current that can quickly tow an unsuspecting swimmer away from the beach.

Rip currents are short-lived and die out usually within 50 to 100 yards of the beach. Anyone caught in a rip current should simply ride with it until it loses its power, or swim slowly out of it to either side as the current begins to dissipate. Swimmers who attempt to swim against the rip to return to their original entry point on the beach usually tire themselves to the point of exhaustion—a life-threatening condition in high surf. Rip currents are a leading cause of the drownings and near-drownings that occur every year on Hawaiian beaches.

Rip currents can be recognized from the beach by watching their effect on incoming waves. Strong rips flowing through the surf zone override and flatten incoming waves. At sandy beaches, rip currents resemble small discolored rivers as they carry sand, foam, and other suspended debris seaward.

Undertows

To most swimmers the terms undertow and rip current are synonymous and are used interchangeably. The undertow phenomenon, however, occurs only when a strong rip current travels directly into large, incoming surf. The rip current will continue to flow seaward as the waves pass over it, causing a swimmer caught in the rip to feel as though he is being pulled down, or towed, underwater.

Undertows are common at the edge of steeply sloped beaches where backwash from a wave can pick up considerable force as it flows back into the ocean, creating a small, localized rip current. A swimmer or stroller caught in the backwash will also feel that he is being pulled underwater if the backwash meets a large breaking wave at the water's edge.

Dangerous Marine Animals

To the delight of beachcombers, tidepoolers, snorkelers, skin divers, and scuba divers, the ocean surrounding the Hawaiian Islands abounds with fish and other marine life. Some marine animals, however, have pincers, teeth, or poisonous stingers, and others are protected by built-in defenses such as spines, thorns, or bristles. While none of Hawai'i's marine animals are normally aggressive toward people, chance encounters with them may lead to injury. The following are some of the potentially dangerous animals in the marine environment.

Cone Shells

As their name implies, cone shells are conically shaped and are usually decorated with brown or black patterns. The snails that inhabit the shells have a poisonous "dart" which is used to inject venom to paralyze or kill their prey. To be on the safe side, do not handle any live cone shells.

In case of a wound, soak and clean the puncture in hot, but not scalding, water for 15 to 90 minutes. Then consult a physician. In the event of any unusual symptoms indicating an allergic reaction, take the victim immediately to the nearest emergency medical facility.

Corals

Coral reefs, common in most Hawaiian waters, account for many of the abrasions and lacerations suffered by swimmers, divers, and surfers. Some of the common stony corals have sharp, crumbling edges that are covered with slime. Cuts from such corals are very susceptible to infection and often slow to heal. Contrary to popular belief, coral lodged in a cut will not continue to grow, but it must be removed because of the high risk of infection. Clean such cuts thoroughly with soap, water, and hydrogen peroxide, and apply an antiseptic as soon as possible.

Portuguese Man-o'-War

The Portuguese man-o'-war is a floating marine jelly-fish, 1–4 inches long, that resembles a translucent, crested, blue bubble. Propelled by wind and currents, the man-o'-war has a retractable, thread-thin tentacle that is trailed underwater to snare food. Each tentacle contains thousands of minute poison-filled stinging cells that paralyze tiny fish and other prey it encounters. The tentacle needs only to brush against a swimmer's skin to cause a burning pain. If it remains in contact with any part of the body, such as the neck, arm, or leg, it delivers a severe, painful sting. The stinging cells retain their toxicity for many hours after the organism is dead, so even a dried-up man-o'-war on the beach should be handled carefully.

The most effective way to remove man-o'-war tentacles from the skin is to rub them off gently with a soft cloth soaked in undiluted vinegar—except, of course, for sensitive areas such as the eyes. Vinegar retards further discharge of venom by the stinging cells. Then the affected area should be rubbed with unseasoned meat tenderizer, a substance that helps neutralize the poison. Some island residents make a paste of vinegar and unseasoned meat tenderizer and keep a jar of of the mixture in the car for first-aid use.

If vinegar and unseasoned meat tenderizer are not available, the traditional island method of removing the tentacles is to rub them gently with wet sand while immersing the affected area in the ocean. The sand quickly breaks up the tentacles and saves the helping hand from getting stung. Most physicians do not advocate this method because sand is abrasive and excessive scrubbing of the skin in an effort to reduce the stinging may cause increased inflammation. However, if the wet sand method is done properly—that is, gently in water—it provides immediate first aid and may be preferable to leaving the tentacles on the skin.

Man-o'-war stings, like those of certain insects, can cause acute reactions in people who are allergic to venom. If any unusual symptoms are observed, take the victim to the nearest emergency medical facility.

Eels

Eels live in crevices in the reef and under coral heads where they feed on fish, crabs, and other similar forms of marine life. They have powerful jaws and many sharp teeth that can inflict serious wounds or even amputate fingers. Tidepool enthusiasts and divers should never reach into holes or cracks where these animals may be living. Fingers may be mistaken for food.

Eels are not usually aggressive unless they are confronted or threatened. They may be observed without fear—but leave them alone. Eel bites may become infected from bacteria on the animal's teeth or in the surrounding sea water. In case of a severe wound, apply direct pressure to stop the bleeding, and take the victim to the nearest emergency medical facility.

Sharks

Sharks are common in Hawaiian waters, but usually do not pose a threat to swimmers. If you should meet a shark face-to-face, try to keep it in view at all times and swim smoothly and steadily to safety. Do not make any erratic or thrashing motions that might be interpreted as signs of panic. In case of a severe wound, apply direct pressure to stop the bleeding, and take the victim to the nearest emergency medical facility.

Spiny Sea Urchins

Spiny sea urchins, commonly known by the Hawaiian term, *wana,* are found in all Hawaiian waters. They are covered with sharp, brittle, needle-like spines that protect the animals from predators. The slightest contact with the spines causes them to break off and embed themselves in the skin. Extensive puncturing from the spines causes an immediate, intense, throbbing pain and swelling that may last for several hours. Pain relief may be obtained by soaking the affected area in hot water. Monitor the victim carefully for signs of shock.

The slender, brittle spines are not easily removed, even with a needle. Most will dissolve if left alone for several weeks, but thicker spines may have to be removed by a physician. Keep the puncture wounds clean and watch for infection.

Ocean Recreation Activities

Swimming

Swimming is the most popular water activity in Hawai'i. Good swimming opportunities exist at almost any near-shore site that offers protection from the prevailing currents and winds. Most people prefer to swim at sandy beaches where sunbathing is more comfortable and where it is easy to walk in and out of the water with bare feet. Kaua'i has many miles of beautiful white sand beaches.

Snorkeling and Nearshore Scuba Diving

The nearshore waters that surround Kaua'i offer a wide variety of marine life and spectacular underwater terrain. Some of the world's most exciting snorkeling and scuba diving sites are found around the island. In addition, island waters are warm throughout the year, and most scuba divers are comfortable with only a wetsuit jacket. Novice snorkelers and scuba divers can arrange for lessons and equipment rentals through beach concessions, tour desks, and dive shops.

Surfing

Kaua'i has some of the best surfing sites in Hawai'i, from the small beginners' breaks on the south shore to the high-surf, for-experts-only breaks on the north shore. Surfers unfamiliar with the island should check with a beach service desk or a local surf shop for information on suitable sites, instruction, and equipment rental.

Bodysurfing and Bodyboarding

Bodysurfing and bodyboarding are very similar wave-riding sports, often practiced at the same location. A bodysurfer uses only his body to ride and manuever on a wave. A bodyboarder lies prone on a small foam body-board that supports his upper body weight. For both sports a pair of swimming fins gives added propulsion for catching waves.

Both sports are very popular because good rides can be found in almost any size of surf, and only a minimum of inexpensive, portable, and easily secured equipment is needed. Fins and bodyboards may be rented at beach concessions or purchased at many sport shops and department stores.

Windsurfing

Windsurfing, the sport of riding a surfboard powered by a sail, was developed in Southern California in the late 1960s and has become an internationally popular form of water recreation. The sport was introduced to Hawai'i in the early 1970s and is firmly established on all the major islands.

The Hawaiian Islands are considered one of the best windsurfing locations in the world. The always-warm waters, the ever-present trade winds, and the challenging Hawaiian surf attract enthusiasts from all over the world to try Hawai'i's open-ocean windsurfing.

References

Abbot, Agatin, E. Alison Kay, Charles Lamoureau, and William Theobald. "Natural Landmarks Survey of the Hawaiian Islands." Prepared for the National Park Service Natural Landmarks Program, Department of the Interior. Departments of Botany and Zoology, University of Hawaii, Honolulu, July 1981.

AECOS, Inc. "Kaua'i Island Coastal Resource Inventory." Prepared for U.S. Army Engineer Division, Pacific Ocean, AECOS Contract No. DACW84-82-C-0016, Kailua, 1982.

Aikin, Ross C. *Kilauea Point Lighthouse, the Landfall Beacon on the Orient Run.* Lihue: Kilauea Point Natural History Association, 1988.

Anders, Gary C. "Native Hawaiian Rights in a Regulated Fishery: An Exploratory Analysis." Research paper prepared for the National Marine Fisheries Service, Honolulu Laboratory, and the Pacific Islands Development Program, East-West Center, Honolulu, August 1987.

Archaeological Research Center of Kauai, Inc. "Archaeological Reconnaissance of Ninini Point Area, Kalapaki, Puna, Kaua'i Island." ARCH 14-176, Lawai, 1980.

Armitage, George, and Henry Judd. *Ghost Dog and Other Hawaiian Legends.* Honolulu: Advertiser Publishing Co., 1944.

Baldwin, Cynthia, Miles Nagata, and David Takeuchi. "Kauai Coastal Zone Resource Survey of Kee, Hanalei, Poipu, and Nualolo Kai." Marine Option Program, University of Hawaii-Hilo, January 1977.

Barrow, Terence. *Captain Cook in Hawaii.* Norfolk Island, Australia: Island Heritage, 1978.

Bennet, Wendell Clark. *Archaeology of Kauai.* Honolulu: Bernice P. Bishop Museum, 1931. Reprint. New York: Kraus Reprint Co., 1976.

Blackman, Dorothy. "The Legend of Barking Sands." *Paradise of the Pacific,* vol. 48, no. 2 (Feb. 1936).

Bolton, H. Carrington. "Some Hawaiian Pastimes." *Journal of American Folklore,* vol. 4, no. 12 (Jan/Mar 1891), pp. 21–26.

Bordner, Richard. "Cultural Reconnaissance Report for Kekaha Beach Shore Protection." Archaeological Research Center Hawaii, Honolulu, 1977.

Carroll, Rick. "Islands in the Sun: Niihau." *Sunday Star-Bulletin & Advertiser,* July 12, 1987.

Ching, Francis, Stephen Palama, and Catherine Stauder. "The Archaeology of Kona, Kaua'i, Na Ahupua'a Weliweli, Pa'a, Maha'ulepu." Archaeological Research Center Hawaii, Lawai, 1974.

Cleghorn, Paul. "Archaeological Reconnaissance Survey of Princeville Lands, Hanalei, Kauai." Manuscript, Department of Anthropology, Bernice P. Bishop Museum, Honolulu, 1979.

Corps of Engineers, U.S. Army Engineer Division, Pacific Ocean. "Hawaii Regional Inventory of the National Shoreline Study." Corps of Engineers, Honolulu, 1971.

Cox, D. C., and L. C. Gordon. "Estuarine Pollution in the State of Hawaii." Volume 1. "Statewide Study." Technical Report no. 31, Water Resources Research Center, University of Hawaii, Honolulu, 1970.

Daws, Gavan. *Shoal of Time.* New York: Macmillan, 1968. Reprint. Honolulu: The University Press of Hawaii, 1974.

Durkin, Pat. *The Kaua'i Guide to Beaches, Water Activities and Safety.* Lihue: Magic Fishes Press, 1988.

Elbert, Samuel, and Noelani Mahoe. *Nā Mele o Hawai'i Nei, 101 Hawaiian Songs.* Honolulu: University of Hawaii Press, 1970.

Emory, Kenneth P. "Ruins at Kee, Haena, Kauai." *Thrum's Hawaiian Annual*. Honolulu: Thos. G. Thrum, 1929.

Emory, Tiare. "Hawaiian Life in Kalalau, Kauai, According to John Hanohano and his Mother, Wahine-i-Keouli Pa." Manuscript, Bishop Museum Archives, Honolulu, 1949.

Farley, F. K. "The Pictured Ledge of Kauai." *Thrum's Hawaiian Annual for 1898*. Honolulu: Thos. G. Thrum, 1898.

Forbes, David. *Queen Emma and Lawai*. Lihue: Kauai Historical Society, 1970.

Fornander, Abraham. "Hawaiian Antiquities and Folklore." *Bernice P. Bishop Museum Memoirs,* vol. 5. Honolulu, 1918.

Gartley, A. "The Wainiha Electric Power Plant." *Thrum's Hawaiian Annual for 1908*. Honolulu: Thos. G. Thrum, 1908.

Gentry, Dick. "Getting Down to Business on Hawaii's 'Forbidden Island.' " *Hawaii Business,* vol. 33, no. 1. (July 1987), p. 56.

Gibbs, James A. *Shipwrecks in Paradise: An Informal Marine History of the Hawaiian Islands*. Seattle: Superior Publishing Co., 1977.

Gilman, G. D. "Journal of a Canoe Voyage along the Kauai Palis, Made in 1845." Hawaii Historical Society Papers no. 14 (1908), pp. 3–8.

Hadley, T. H., and M. S. Williams. *The New Kauai. Garden Island of Hawai'i*. Lihue: Kauai Publishing Co., 1967.

Handy, E. S. Craighill, Elizabeth Handy, and Mary Kawena Pukui. *Native Planters in Old Hawaii*. Bishop Museum Bulletin 233. Honolulu, 1972.

Hinds, Norman. *The Geology of Kauai and Niihau*. Honolulu: Bernice P. Bishop Museum, 1930. Reprint. New York: Kraus Reprint Co., 1971.

Horowitz, Lenore. *Kauai, 1988–89 Underground Guide*. Atherton, CA: Papaloa Press, 1988.

Hulme, Kathryn. *The Robert Allerton Story*. Kauai: John Gregg Allerton, 1979.

Johnson, Rubellite K. *Kūkini 'Aha'ilono*. Honolulu: Topgallant Publishing Co., 1976.

Jones, Stella M. Papers, 1928-1950. Unpublished papers from Kauai field trips. Bernice P. Bishop Museum Library, Honolulu.

Kamakau, Samuel. *Ka Po'e Kahiko, the People of Old*. Bernice P. Bishop Museum Special Publication 51. Honolulu, 1964.

Kauai Bicentenial Committee. *Waimea, Island of Kauai, 1778-1978*. Waimea: Kauai Bicentennial Committee, 1977.

Kay, E. Alison, et al. "The Composition of Micromoluscan Assemblages in the Hawaiian Archipelago: Niihau, French Frigate Shoals and Kure." National Science Foundation Grant for Undergraduate Research Participation and Office of Marine Affairs Coordinator, State of Hawaii, Honolulu, March 1982.

Kelly, Marion, Clayton Hee, and Ross Cordy. "Cultural Reconnaissance of Hydroelectric Plant Sites, Waihe'e Valley, Maui and Lumaha'i Valley, Kaua'i." Manuscript, Department of Anthropology, Bernice P. Bishop Museum, Honolulu, 1978.

Kelsey, Theodore. "Kaua'i Place Names." Unpublished manuscript, Kelsey Collection, Hawaii State Archives, n.d.

Kikuchi, William. "Archaeological Reconnaissance Survey of the Keoneloa Bay Area." Kauai Community College, Lihue, May 14, 1980.

————. "Assessment of Damage to Historical and Archaeological Resources Resulting from Hurricane 'Iwa to Kaua'i County, 50–30–10–80, Po'ipū, Koloa District, Island of Kauai." Kauai Community College, Lihue, 1983.

————. "Rainbow Petroglyph Site." *Archaeology on Kaua'i,* vol. 10, no. 1 (February 1983). Anthropology Club of Kaua'i Community College, Lihue.

————. "Survey Report: Underwater Communications Project, Nohili Ditch Area, Pacific Missile Range Facility, District of Waimea, Island of Kaua'i." Kauai Community College, Lihue, Oct. 15, 1979.

Knudsen, Eric A. "Some Personal Experiences on the Na Pali Coast." Paper presented at Kauai Historical Society meeting, May 27, 1940, Lihue, Kauai.

Lindquist, Carl. *The Musicians*. Norfolk Island, Australia: Island Heritage, 1971.

Lynch, Kay. "Big Changes Backed for Little Niihau School." *Honolulu Advertiser,* Saturday, March 7, 1987.

Madden, W. D., and C. L. Paulsen. "The Potential for Mullet and Milkfish Culture in Hawaiian Fishponds." State of Hawaii, Department of Planning and Economic Development, Honolulu, 1977.

Macdonald, Gordon A., Agatin T. Abbott, and Frank L. Peterson. *Volcanoes in the Sea,* 2nd ed., Honolulu: University of Hawaii Press, 1983.

Macdonald, Gordon A., Dan A. Davis, and Doak C. Cox. *Geology and Groundwater Resources of the Island of Kauai, Hawaii*. Honolulu: State of Hawaii Division of Hydrography, 1960.

McCoy, Patrick "Archaeological Research at Fort Elizabeth, Waimea, Kauai, Hawaiian Islands: Phase I." Department of Anthropology, Report no. 72-7, Bernice P. Bishop Museum, Honolulu, 1972.

McDonald, Marie A. *Ka Lei, the Leis of Hawaii*. Honolulu: Topgallant Publishing Co. and Press Pacifica, 1985.

Malo, David. *Hawaiian Antiquities*. Bernice P. Bishop Museum Special Publication 2. Honolulu, 1951.

Markrich, Mike. "The Only Fish in the Sea." *Honolulu,* vol. 22, no. 12, (June 1988).

Moriarty, Linda Paik. *Ni'ihau Shell Leis*. Honolulu: University of Hawaii Press, 1986.

National Oceanic and Atmospheric Administration, U.S. Department of Commerce. "United States Coast Pilot 7: Pacific Coast—California, Oregon, Washington, and Hawaii." NOAA: Washington, D.C., 1977.

Pickard, Robert. "Poipu of Yesteryear." *Sunday Star-Bulletin & Advertiser,* August 26, 1979.

Pratt, H. Douglas, Phillip Bruner, and Delwyn Berrett. *The Birds of Hawaii and the Tropical Pacific*. Princeton, N.J.: Princeton University Press, 1987.

Pukui, Mary Kawena. *'Ōlelo No'eau, Hawaiian Proverbs and Poetical Sayings*. Bernice P. Bishop Museum Special Publication no. 71. Honolulu, 1983.

Pukui, Mary, and Alfons Korn. *The Echo of Our Song*. Honolulu: University of Hawaii Press, 1979.

Rho, Marguerite. "Wainiha Linemen." *Ampersand,* Fall 1988. Alexander & Baldwin, Inc., Honolulu.

Rice, William Hyde. *Hawaiian Legends*. Bernice P. Bishop Museum Special Publication 63. Honolulu, 1977.

Riley, Thomas J., and Karma Ibsen-Riley. *Taylor Camp, Hawaii. The Life and Death of a Hippie Community*. Field Museum of Natural History Bulletin, June 1979.

Riznik, Barnes. *Wai'oli Mission House*. Lihue: Grove Farm and Waioli Mission House, 1987.

Schmidt, Robert J. "The Population of Northern Kauai in 1847." *Hawai'i Historical Review,* vol. 2, no. 3 (1966), pp. 303–304.

Sinoto, Aki. Archaeological Reconnaissance Survey of Knudsen Trust Lands at Koloa, Poipu, Kauai. Manuscript, Department of Anthropology, Bernice P. Bishop Museum, Honolulu, 1975.

Smith, Walter J. *Legends of Wailua*. Lihue: Kauai Printers, 1955.

Stacey, Mary K. "Na Pali Coast Trip—Kauai, 1953." Manuscript, Bernice P. Bishop Museum, Honolulu. Photocopy.

Stroup, Elaine S. (Propellor Club of the United States, Port of Honolulu). *Ports of Hawaii*. Honolulu: Red Dot Publishing Co., 1950.

Sutherland, Audrey. *Paddling Hawai'i*. Seattle: The Mountaineers, 1988.

Tabrah, Ruth M. *Ni'ihau, the Last Hawaiian Island*. Kailua: Press Pacifica, 1987.

TenBruggencate, Jan. "A Lost Tribe, a Lonely Valley—A Legend from Kauai." *Sunday Star-Bulletin & Advertiser,* October 6, 1985.

———. "Niihau Today." *Honolulu Advertiser,* January 23, 1986.

———. "Paradise Lost on Kauai." *Honolulu Advertiser,* March 11, 1980.

Thurston, Lorrin P. "The Kingdom of Nualolo." *Honolulu Advertiser,* July 20, 1922.

Tomonari-Tuggle, Myra Jean F. "An Archaeological Reconnaissance Survey: Na Pali Coast State Park, Island of Kauai." State of Hawaii, Department of Land and Natural Resources, Division of State Parks, Honolulu, 1979.

Twain-Kate, Gregory. "How the Hawaiians of Niihau are Protected from Progress." *Spirit of Aloha Magazine,* Jan/Feb 1980, Honolulu.

U.S. Army Corps of Engineers, Pacific Ocean Division. "Hawaii National Inventory of the National Shoreline Study." Honolulu, 1971.

Valier, Kathy. *On the Nā Pali Coast*. Honolulu: University of Hawaii Press, 1988.

Waldman, Alan. "The House on the Hill." *Honolulu,* March 1983.

Wenkam, Robert. *Hawaii's Garden Island: Kauai*. Chicago, New York, San Francisco: Rand McNally, 1979.

Whitney, Henry. *The Hawaiian Guide Book*. 1875. Reprint. Rutland, VT, and Tokyo: Charles E. Tuttle Co., 1970.

———. *Tourist's Guide Through Hawaii*. Honolulu: Hawaiian Gazette Co., 1890.

Williams, Paul Koki. "Ni'ihau Dialect." *Archaeology on Kaua'i,* vol. 9, no. 3 (September 1982).

Yent, Martha. "Archaeological Monitoring, Mapping, and Testing of Sites in Hanakapi'ai Valley, Na Pali Coast, Kauai." State of Hawaii, DLNR, Division of States Parks, Honolulu, 1981.

———. "Archaeological Monitoring, Mapping, and Testing of Sites in Kalalau Valley, Na Pali Coast, Kauai." State of Hawaii, DLNR, Division of State Parks, Honolulu, 1981.

———. "Archaeological Mapping: Nualolo Aina, Na Pali Coast, Kauai." State of Hawaii, DLNR, Division of State Parks, Honolulu, 1983.

Yim, Susan. "Jewels of the Pacific." *Honolulu Star-Bulletin,* Thursday, September 16, 1982.

Yoneyama, Tom. "Battle Over Barking Sands." *Hawaii Business,* vol. 33, no. 1 (July 1987), p. 46.

Index

Access, shoreline, xi, 6, 51, 58, 90
Ahukini State Recreation Pier, 5
Akaka, Senator Daniel, 23
Alexander, Rev. William, 30
'Aliomanu Beach, 14
Allerton, John, 40, 64
Anahola Beach Park, 14
'Anini Beach Park, 24

Barking Sands, 49, 75
Beach House Beach, 66
Black Pot Beach Park, 27
Boat ramps, 2, 3, 9, 11, 25, 29
Bodyboarding, 107
Bodysurfing, 107
Brennecke Beach, 71

Camp Naue, 36
Cook, Captain James, 55, 90, 92, 95
Corals, 104
Crater Hill, 22, 23, 92

Davidson Beach, 53
Donkey Beach, 12

Eels, 105
'Ele'ele, 59, 64
Emma, Queen, 26

Fishing, traditional methods of, 2, 6, 11,
    19, 24, 27, 33, 34, 35, 36, 43, 62, 64, 87
Fishponds, 2, 62
Fort Alexander, 27
Fort Elizabeth State Historical Park, 56

Gillin's Beach, 74
Glass Beach, 60

Hā'ena Beach Park, 36
Hā'ena State Park, 37
Hanakapi'ai Beach, 40, 103

Hanalei, 43
Hanalei Pavilion Beach Park, 29
Hanamā'ulu Beach Park, 6, 38
Hanapēpē Beach Park, 59
Ha'ula Beach, 74
Hawaiian Canneries Company, 9
Heiau, 3, 5, 9, 18, 20, 21, 37, 40, 61
Honopū Beach, 40, 44
Horner, Albert, 9
Hule'ia National Wildlife Refuge, 2
Hurricane 'Iwa, 4, 60, 67, 71, 72

Infinities, 56
Inouye, Senator Daniel, 23

Ka'aka'aniu, 15, 18, 19
Ka'aku'u Beach, 81, 84, 102
Kāhili Beach, 19, 21
Kalāheo, 61
Kalākaua, King David, 67
Kalalau Beach, 40, 42, 44, 103
Kalaniana'ole, Prince Jonah Kuhio, 67
Kalaoa Beach, 99
Kalapakī Beach, 3
Kalihiwai Beach, 24
Kamalino Beach, 95, 102
Kamehameha I, 27, 56
Kamehameha II, 30
Kamehameha IV, 26
Kamehameha V, 26
Kanoa, Paul, 2
Kapa'a Beach Park, 10
Kapi'olani, Queen Lydia, 67
Kauapea Beach, 23
Ka'ula, 82, 95
Kauwaha Beach, 86
Kawaihoa, 82, 93, 94, 95, 96
Kawailoa, 74, 75
Keālia Beach, 11, 103
Keamano Beach, 84
Keanahaki Beach, 96, 100, 102

Keawanui Beach, 84
Kē'ē Beach, 37, 38, 39, 40, 41, 42
Ke'elikolani, Princess Ruth, 4
Kekaha, 49, 51, 52
Kekaha Beach Park, 52
Keoneloa, 72
Kepuhi, 35
Ki'eki'e Beach, 89, 92
Ki'i Landing, 83, 101, 102
Kīkīaola Small Boat Harbor, 53
Kīlauea Point National Wildlife Refuge,
    16, 20, 22
Kīpū Kai, 76
Knudsen, Valdemar, 69
Kōloa Landing, 68
Ko'olau School, 16
Kukui'ula Small Boat Harbor, 65

Lanipuao Rock, 64
Larsens Beach, 17
Lāwa'i Kai, 64
Legends, 46, 50, 65, 76, 102
Lehua Island, 51, 82, 102
Lehua Landing, 82, 94
Lihu'e Plantation Company, 5, 10, 12, 13,
    14
Lucas, Mary N., 18
Lucy Wright Beach Park, 54
Lumaha'i Beach, 32, 103
Lydgate State Park, 7

McBryde, Alexander, 64
McBryde, Walter, 61
Māhā'ulepū Beach, 73
Majors Bay, 51
Mana Coastal Plain, 49, 50, 51, 52, 53
Miloli'i Beach, 40, 41, 47
Moloa'a Bay, 16

Nā Pali Coast State Park, 37, 40
Nāwiliwili Harbor, 2, 6

113

Nāwiliwili Park, 2
Nāwiliwili Small Boat Harbor, 3
Ni'ihau, xi, 43, 49, 51, 70, 79
Ni'ihau Helicopters, Inc., 81, 98
Ni'ihau shells, 85
Ninini, 4, 5
Niumalu Beach Park, 2
Nomilu Fishpond, 62
Nonopapa Beach, 92, 102
Nu'alolo Kai Beach, 40, 45
Nudists, 5, 14, 24, 75
Nukoli'i Beach Park, 6

Ocean recreation activities, 107

Pacific Missile Range Facility, 50
Pacific Tropical Botanical Garden, 64
Pākalā Beach, Makaweli, 56, 83
Pākalā Point, Moloa'a, 18
Pālama Beach, 62, 64
Pāpa'a Bay, 14, 15, 16
Petroglyphs, 73, 75
Pila'a Beach, 18
Pine Trees, 30
Po'ipū Beach, 68
Po'ipū Beach Park, 70, 71
Pōleho Beach, 99, 100
Polihale State Park, 49, 97, 98, 100
Po'oneone Beach, 98
Port Allen, 53, 59
Portlock, Nathaniel, 87, 92

Portuguese man-o'-war, 104
Prince Kūhiō Park, 67
Princeville, 26
Pueo Point, 99
Pu'uwai Beach, 88

Queens Pond, 50

Rice, William H., 4, 102
Rip currents, 103
Robinson family, Ni'ihau, xi, 43, 56, 87,
    89, 90, 97
Russian forts, 27, 56

Salt Pond Beach Park, 58
Scheffer, Georg Anton, 27, 56
Scuba diving, 107
Seals, 39, 102
Seaweed, gathering, 15, 17, 18, 19
Secret Beach, Kalaheo, 61
Secret Beach, Kilauea, 24
Sharks, 2, 6, 26, 58, 105
Shells, 39, 85, 104
Shipman, Herbert, 77
Shipwreck Beach, 72, 76
Shorebreaks, 103
Snorkeling, 107
Spiny sea urchins, 105
Spouting Horn Beach Park, 64, 65
Surfing, 107
Swimming, 107

Tabrah, Ruth, 90, 95
Taylor Camp, 38
Tsunami, 30, 34
Tunnels Beach, 36

Undertows, 104

Vancouver, George, 73, 87

Wahiawa Bay, 60
Waiakalua Iki Beach, 20
Waiakalua Nui Beach, 21
Waika'ea Canal, 9, 11
Waikoko Beach, 28, 30
Wailua Beach, 8
Wailua River State Park, 9
Waimea, 43, 55
Waimea State Recreation Pier, 54
Wainiha Beach Park, 34
Wai'ōhai, 69
Wai'oli Beach Park, 30
Waipa Stream, 31
Waipouli Beach, 9
Wanini Beach, 25
Waterhouse, John, 76
Waterhouse Beach, 68
Water safety, 103
Whales, 82
Windsurfing, 107
Wyllie, Robert, 26